THE
WINE POCKET
BIBLE

THE
WINE POCKET BIBLE

ANDREW SMITH & JENNY DODD

Note to readers

The vintage charts included in this book give marks out of 100, and each chart excludes 1984, as customary due to the poorness of the year.

This edition first published in Great Britain 2009 by
Crimson Publishing, a division of Crimson Business Ltd.
Westminster House
Kew Road
Richmond
Surrey
TW9 2ND

A catalogue record for this book is available from the British Library.

ISBN 978 1 907087 04 2

Printed and bound by LegoPrint SpA, Trento

CONTENTS

INTRODUCTION

The astounding variety of wines available can seem a little overwhelming at times. Yet, to enjoy a wine you don't necessarily need to know its life story. This book introduces you to some of the nuances of the wine world, so that you can make your own exploration of the tantalising opportunities available. With a little more wine knowledge you may surprise yourself – safe old favourites are soon replaced with exciting new gastronomic discoveries. From wine and food pairing to correct tasting procedure, we will help you get the best out of the galaxy of stunning wines available from across the world. Including tips on buying, cellaring and the health benefits of the noble beverage, *The Wine Pocket Bible* is your trusty companion on a truly enjoyable tour of the world of wine.

⊶ A SHORT HISTORY OF WINE ⊷

By way of introduction, this whirlwind history of wine may serve as a brief indication of how changes have shaped the character of the modern wine industry.

The **Egyptians** planted grapes along the fertile banks of the Nile in 2500BC and were the first to embark on a process which would transcend the legacy of even their own culture. They designed an early wine-press that consisted of a platform upon which the grapes were placed for treading through a mesh, with a vat set underneath to collect the resulting juice and pulped skins.

This mixture of grape flesh, juice, skin and seeds was then put in earthenware pots to ferment, before being siphoned off and filtered ready for drinking. The process is remarkably similar to today.

From humble beginnings as a rustic brew in the land of the Pharaohs, winemaking travelled to its natural home on the Mediterranean and further to the Aegean. In the hands of the **Greeks**, the process of winemaking changed dramatically. They trained grape vines to grow up trellises and planted them in orderly rows, giving birth to the concept of the vineyard. Amazingly, traditional Greek winemaking practices still influence local production of rustic wines with some international appeal. Thucydides remarked that 'The peoples of the Mediterranean began to emerge from barbarism when they learned to cultivate the olive and the vine.' The spread of both the vine and cultivation to Rome was to herald a turn in the fortunes of the Greeks and a shift in historical dialectic.

As power balances readjusted, **Rome** became the world's dominant force and their cultural hegemony stamped itself across early Europe. So too did their winemaking, and the land of cultivated vines, termed 'Oenotria' by the Greeks, exhibited the greatest innovations in winemaking since its conception. As the imperial eagle of Rome spread across Europe, so too did the vine. Roman settlers cultivated vines in Britain, France, Germany and beyond, impressing their methods on local populations who would come to make their own wines.

The eventual decline of Rome's influence did not herald the death of winemaking, and locals took over control of production. Wine production flourished for a time in the Middle East and North Africa, before it was checked by the spread of Islam which forbade intoxication. In France and Germany, however, monks and religious orders became some of the most prodigious wine producers as Christian sacraments virtually demanded libations. They produced rustic wines for use in church and distributed wine to help fund the abbeys. Throughout the **Middle Ages** wine was a popular and widely available drink, varying widely in quality and price as it does today. From the courts of kings to London ale-houses, wine enchanted and intoxicated myriad drinkers, thinkers and thieves.

The social advances witnessed in the **Early Modern** period rev-olutionised lives across Europe. The rise of artisanal bourgeois classes turned winemaking into a skilled pursuit practised by enterprising businessmen in the Renaissance states of Italy. Likewise, an appreciation of fine wine developed.

Under Elizabeth I, the expansion of Britain's merchant navy saw widespread trade links with Portugal and Spain established and wine freely traded with them for the first time. The use of glass to bottle wine began in the 17th century, and this improved both the quality and ability to transport and store individual bottles, as opposed to the casks previously used. Perhaps the greatest change to this was that some Europeans now conducted their business and pleasure outwith Europe itself in a so-called **New World**. Fearful that lush new worlds and cities of gold would lose their lustre without recourse to familiar wine, conquistadors brought with them samples of their native vines and attempted to grow them in a hostile climate. Most did poorly and the New World would remain obscure in the wine world until much later. Nevertheless, the seed had been planted.

The 18th century saw the development of distinguishable grape varieties, as French and German wine-growers established the tenets of the modern classification systems by developing distinct regional wines. This distinction heralded the birth of a wine industry worth speaking of – as private individuals began increas-ingly to import and export wines of some recognised quality. The rise of the industry was fed by something of a golden age in European wine, as the beginning of the 1800s failed to halt the popularity and availability of fine wine at all the best dinner tables in Europe.

The 19th century, however, held a massive shock in store for the European wine industry. Travel to and from the Americas brought a pestilential louse back to France. *Phylloxera vastatrix* (a kind of root louse) claimed the vines and livelihood of most of Europe's wine regions during a period beginning in the 1860s as it spread like wildfire. Solutions were difficult to come by, yet were eventually found: cuttings of the European vine were grafted onto the rootstock of the American vines, which were not affected by the louse, allowing for the winemaking potential of the European grape to be augmented by a resistance to this new outbreak. Replanting was swift and large scale, with very few places in Europe unaffected. This solution also resulted in the successful cultivation of European vines in North America, resulting in a boom in New World production.

The wars of the 20th century blighted many vineyards, whilst devastating the production of traditional growers in France, Germany, Italy and elsewhere. Much wine was, however, produced for soldiers, ensuring the survival of a diminished wine economy. The spread of unionisation as a concept also led to the increasing appearance of **cooperative wineries** – first in the Languedoc-Roussillon then the rest of France and the world. **Technological advancement** likewise changed the wine industry. From tractors to irrigation methods to stainless steel wineries, the making of wine progressed immeasurably.

The '**Judgement of Paris**' in 1976 was a turning point in the history of wine. It represented the moment at which the New World came of age, gaining a critical reputation it had lacked until that point. An international wine tasting organised in Paris pitted the wines of California against those of France. Californian Cabernet Sauvignons were set alongside Bordeaux Châteaux, and Californian Chardonnays were set alongside Burgundian classics. The wines were submitted to a panel of 11 judges (one from Britain, one from the USA and nine from France) for blind tasting and analysis. In a surprising result, California triumphed, with an American wine being ranked highest on average in both red and white categories. Without doubt the results revolutionised the wine market – greatly increasing the demand for New World wines and forcing some introspection on behalf of the French. The results have always been controversial due to the subjectivity of individual tasters but the results were enough of a shock to alter the modern wine market forever. This test was instrumental in the increasing global nature of the wine market and the forerunner of today's surfeit of imported international varieties.

The new international wine world, with 'Flying winemakers' and global consultants has changed the nature of wine production. In Argentina, Chile and other such countries standards have been improved as experienced winemakers have brought new methodology to traditional production. However, the **globalisation** of the market has also challenged some, who believe the identity of the varied wine regions is challenged by dominant consumer markets which respond to articulate critics. Debate over the concept of '**Parkerisation**' has characterised this discourse, with international vineyards responding to the preferences of the influential American critic Robert Parker to ensure better reviews and therein better sales. Likewise, investment by companies such as Mondavi has been resisted by French winegrowers as 'Dollar imperialism'. These emotionally charged terms over-simplify the debate, as a changing wine market offers both the opportunities and drawbacks that cyclical changes in climate have historically brought. The USA has led a **consumer revolution** which has revitalised the wine market since the 1970s, by focusing on accessibility and market demands rather than staunch adherence to tradition. However, within the Old World of European vineyards there is likewise innovation alongside superlative tradition. Many of these wines have a centuries-old history simply because they merit one. Neither New nor Old has triumphed and victory belongs only to the wine-lover and his cellar.

Wine at times seems a substance bound to baffle. At the heart of the matter, however, is an irreducibly pleasurable beverage bound up only in the vocabulary of effusive praise. Amongst ACs, DOCGs and IGTs there lies merely a promise to the drinker: you've found what you're looking for. If anything, this book is intended to display openness, and an accepting attitude to the wines of every region of the world. Consider then this book as a corkscrew: a map through vineyards, an ally in the cellar and a guide at awkward moments of indecision.

'In vino veritas'
Pliny

HOW WINE IS MADE

'Making good wine is a skill. Fine wine is an art.'
Robert Mondavi

This section will show you the ins and outs of how wine is made, bridging the vast gap between the grape and the wine sitting in your glass.

⊶ FACTORS AFFECTING ⊷ GRAPE-GROWING

LATITUDE

The majority of the world's wine is produced in regions that lie between the latitudes of 30° and 50°. This is because the temperate climate in this band, which usually stays between 50°F and 70°F throughout the year, provides ideal conditions in which to grow all varieties.

SOIL TYPE

The soil type is extremely important and influences the amount of minerals and nutrients that the vine is exposed to, supports the root structure and controls the drainage potential. Vines grow best on well-drained soil and 'damp feet' can ruin the potential for good wine. Poor soil, which often would not support other crops, encourages the vine to send its roots deep into the mineral rich sub-soil and encourages less fruit with more concentrated juice. Vines grown in rich soil tend to produce too much fruit with little concentration of juice – this in turn leads to a poor-quality wine.

Viticulture

The job of a viticulturist is a busy one, entailing numerous duties such as monitoring the development of the fruit in order to ascertain the optimum time to harvest the crop, fertilising the vines, preventing or controlling the spread of pests and diseases, and ongoing maintenance of the vines.

CLIMATE

Many vineyards are planted on sloping ground as this provides both a natural means of drainage for the vines and also helps to control the sunlight they receive throughout the year.

- In cooler climates, vineyards are usually located on a south facing slope as this increases the strength of sunlight and maximises the hours of sunshine they are exposed to during the summer growing season.

- In warmer climates, planting vineyards on a north facing slope is favoured as they offer some protection against overexposure to the potentially scorching rays of the sun.

The presence of lakes and mountain ranges can also be beneficial, as they help to create a stable microclimate for the vines to grow in.

The importance of *terroir*

The French have a standard phrase that encompasses the interplay of soil type, climate and grape variety – this is terroir. *This term, which has no English equivalent, describes a belief in how the unique nuances of a wine's upbringing influence its eventual quality. Ideally,* terroir *represents a marriage of ideal conditions for the cultivation of a particular grape, which leads to an excellent wine.*

AGE

The best grapes tend to come from the oldest vines, which have a life span of centuries. In Europe, however, there are few vines which pre-date the *Phylloxera* epidemic, although there are some 100-year-old vines in the USA and Australia. As vines age, they produce lower yields of fruit with extremely concentrated juice – ideal for the winemaker.

'Good wine is a good familiar creature if it be well used.'
William Shakespeare, Othello, II. iii.

⊶ VINIFICATION ⊷

Vinification concerns the process of creating fine wines from raw grapes within a winery. This process generally takes place along the following lines.

PRESSING

Harvested grapes are collected and delivered to the winery in order to begin separating the liquid and solid parts of the grape by pressing. During pressing, grape clusters are placed between two surfaces and gradually squeezed in order to extract as much juice as possible. The product of this initial pressing stage is called must, a juice that still contains the skin and the seeds of the grapes.

Pocket fact ♀

Although this varies widely depending on pressing methods and grapes used, as a general rule one kilogram of grapes will yield about one 75cl bottle of wine.

FERMENTATION

Fermentation turns the sugars in the grape juice into alcohol by adding yeast. Occasionally, a winemaker may wish to stop fermentation early if he wants to produce a sweet or medium-dry wine. Roughly speaking, every gram of sugar that is converted during fermentation will produce about half a gram of alcohol.

It is at this stage when variation creeps into the process of wine-making, so we shall take a look at the nuances of red, white and rosé wines.

Red wine

The rich colours and deep flavours that characterise red wine are created from grape skins. Tannins, which give reds a well-rounded, robust flavour and create dark, luminous colours are also present in the skins. Because of this, contact between the juice and the skins is essential during both the pressing and fermentation processes. The main techniques for producing red wine are:

● **Pumping over** (*remontage*): Wine from the bottom of the fermenting vat is drawn up and pumped back over the top of the contents. This ensures good consistent contact with the skins and breaks up any crust that has formed at the top of the vat, helping to ensure a wine is tannic and well coloured.

- A **fermenting juice** can also be drawn off to increase the proportion of solids (grape skins) to liquid and ensure a robust flavour. The wine drawn off is often fermented and bottled separately as rosé. This is common in California, where powerful red Zinfandel is produced using this method and the off-shoot is a light, fruity white Zinfandel rosé.

- **Carbonic maceration** is another variation on traditional fermentation. In this process, whole bunches of grapes are placed in the vat underneath a layer of carbon dioxide. Fermentation occurs within the grapes, which burst and release a lot of colour but little tannin. This process is generally used to produce soft and very fruity reds intended for early drinking.

Rosé wine

Most rosés are produced by allowing mid-length contact with the skins during fermentation (typically two to three days), but there are also two other ways in which rosé wines can be produced:

- **Saignée:** Grapes are de-stalked but not crushed before being vatted for 12 and 24 hours. After this the juice is run off for fermentation without further skin contact.

- **Blending:** Mixing red wine into white to impart colour is an extremely uncommon practice and is illegal in most European wine-growing regions.

White wine

White wines are light in colour because the skins are removed from the must within a few hours of pressing. Because of this initial separation, whites have considerably lower amounts of tannin. Fermentation takes place at lower temperatures and over a longer period than with red wine, to ensure concentration of fruit flavours combined with lightness of colour.

MATURATION

After fermentation, the winemaker is left with a rough wine not yet ready for the public. Although most wines are made for youthful drinking, finer wines generally benefit from some period of maturation in either cask or bottle. Maturation encourages a gentle oxidation, changing the character of the wine and adding tannin as it softens other characteristics.

Oak contains tannins that can supplement those in either red or white wine and enrich the flavours of both.

- In red wine, oak tannins infuse a rich woody flavour into the wine and extract overripe fruit aromas.

- In white they replace grassy acidity with complex vanilla and caramel flavours.

Small barrels increase contact with the wood and have a greater effect on the flavour. Different types of oak can influence the taste.

FINING

Before bottling, every wine must undergo some process of fining. Microscopic elements such as proteins and other particles that give wine a cloudy appearance are removed using fining agents such as egg-white. These are added to wine to capture suspended particles and weigh them down to settle at the bottom of the vessel. The wine is then filtered in order to separate it from the sediment that has been collected. Generally, the finer the quality of a wine, the gentler the filtration will be, as unselective filters can damage the character of a wine.

BOTTLING

Wines are bottled in a clean environment to ensure they reach the public in excellent condition. Wines have traditionally been fitted with a cork at this point, to allow bottle-aging, although many wines intended for early drinking are now closed with screw-tops.

DIFFERENT WINE STYLES

Clearly wine is not limited to still red, white and rosé, and some of the more individual wine styles vary from these standard practices.

SWEET WINE

To create a tasty sweet wine, the grape variety needs to maintain high acidity alongside very high levels of ripeness. Commonly used varieties to make sweet wine are Riesling, Gürztraminer and Muscat.

There are three main techniques behind the creation of sweet wines:

- ***Botrytis cinerea* (Noble Rot)**
  This is a spore-like fungus that attacks healthy grapes and spreads over them, feeding on the sugar in the fruit. If the correct temperature combination of damp nights and warming days occurs whilst the grapes are under attack from the fungus, they will naturally dry and dehydrate beneath it, which concentrates their sugar content. Examples of Noble Rot wine are the marvellous Sauternes wines from Château d'Yquem and the famed Tokaij Aszu from Hungary.
- **Eiswein (Ice Wine)**
  Eiswein is made from grapes that have been picked during a hard frost. When these frozen grapes are pressed, the denser concentrated sugars are separated from the frozen water content of the grape to create an extremely sweet must with high acidity. This is increasingly popular in Canada, where

complex and luscious Ice Wine is produced during their cold winters.

- **Late harvesting**
The later grapes are picked, the riper they will be, and if they are left on the vines well into autumn they will ripen to their fullest. Leaving the grapes to dehydrate concentrates their sugars by removing much of the natural water content, creating sweet wines that are full of sticky honey and intense fruit flavours.

FORTIFIED WINE

When making fortified wine, alcohol is added to the must before fermentation is complete; this kills off the yeast and leaves a higher amount of residual sugar in the wine than usual. The end result is wine that is sweeter, with a higher alcohol content of 18%–20%. The most well-known varieties of fortified wine are port, sherry and vermouth.

> *'Wine fills the heart with courage.'*
> Plato

CHAMPAGNE AND SPARKLING WINES

Sparkling wine can legitimately be made from virtually any grape variety, but true Champagne can only be made from Pinot Noir, Chardonnay and Pinot Meunier in the Champagne area of France.

The grapes must be harvested about three to four weeks earlier than usual as it is at this point that the acids are high and the sugars low – optimum levels for creating a sparkling wine. They are then pressed and undergo the same primary fermentation process as that of white wine.

Following primary fermentation, Champagnes and sparkling wines undergo several unique processes.

Blending

This blends together the must from various grape varieties in order to create a pleasing wine. For Champagne, this could be a blend of all the accepted grape varieties, only two, or it could be created from just one. For example, Champagne produced solely from the dark Pinot Noir grape is called Blanc de Noirs (white from black); Champagne produced from Chardonnay alone is known as Blanc de Blancs (white from white).

In reality, a blend is most common and is usually created within guideline perimeters of each winemaker's individual style. This final blended mixture is known as the cuvée.

Second fermentation

The *Méthode Champenoise* is the most well-known and popular bottling process in the production of Champagne and sparkling wines, yielding by far the highest quality results. The cuvée is inserted into each bottle, along with a mixture of wine, yeast and sugar (known as *liquer de triage*) which will encourage the second fermentation in the bottle. The carbon dioxide produced as a by-product gets trapped inside in the form of bubbles. Non-Vintage Champagnes must remain thus for a minimum of 15 months, whilst Vintage Champagnes require *at least* three years.

Dégorgement

Once the bottle of sparkling wine has been left *en triage* for two to four years, it is mature enough to drink. However, the left-over yeast from the fermentation process is still trapped inside in the form of a silty sediment. To get rid of this, each bottle is tipped from a horizontal position to vertical (neck facing downwards) which encourages the sediment to slip down into the tip of the neck (known as *rémuage*). The top inch of the bottle is then rapidly frozen and the cap removed, allowing the natural pressure from the bubbles in the wine to push out the frozen yeast plug (known as *dégorgement*).

Dosage

During the process of *dégorgement*, a little liquid is lost – and this is topped up with a mixture of wine and cane sugar solution. This increases the level of residual sugar in the sparkling wine, and moderates how dry the wine is according to the individual house style. Without this counterbalancing agent, sparkling wines would be incredibly acidic.

Finishing

Finally, a cork and wire hood are placed over the top of the bottle and the wine is left to sit for at least another six months in order to allow the dosage to integrate fully, and to let the wine rest. After that, it's ready to crack open!

Pocket fact ♀

When a bottle of Champagne is opened, the cork flies out at around 25 miles per hour.

ORGANIC AND BIODYNAMIC WINES

Organic and biodynamic wines have grown in popularity over recent years – due to the increasing emphasis on sustainable agriculture and our awareness of pesticides and quest for natural produce.

ORGANIC WINE

All organic wines are produced in adherence with strict standards set out by official regulatory bodies (such as the United States Department of Agriculture in America, or Ecovert in France). But remember, different nations have differing certification criteria, and as such what is classed as organic in one country may not be in another.

Organic viticulture

At a viticultural level, all organic growers dismiss pesticides and insecticides in favour of natural pest control methods. Ingenious ideas include planting blackberry bushes around the perimeter of a vineyard in order to encourage insects that will eat the bugs that prey on the vine leaves, putting up bird boxes to coax them to settle in the area and pick off the pests that eat the grapes, and weeding out unwanted plants by hand or machine.

Sulphites are present in most organic wine as a natural by-product of fermentation. However, their use is kept to a minimum during viticulture and vinification, so that they only reach levels of about a third of that found in conventionally made wines. If sulphites are a real worry, make sure that you buy organic wine from America, where legislation dictates that any wine certified organic will have had no extra sulphites added in the process.

> *'Wine in itself is an excellent thing.'*
> Pope Pius XII Airen

BIODYNAMIC WINE

Biodynamic wine offers a truly ecological approach to winemaking along holistic, sustainable principles. And just like organic wines, they have to meet rigorous criteria set out by third party regulators to be certified as biodynamic.

The theory

In biodynamic winemaking, the timing of operations such as planting and harvesting depend upon lunar cycles and other natural phenomenon. The balance of the soil is carefully maintained through recycling of nutrients and the use of a complex system of herbal sprays and composting techniques. All this creates a harmonious balance between man harvesting the resources of nature without corrupting it, and results are starting to suggest that this holistic approach yields excellent results.

Does it work?

There is no doubt that some methods used in biodynamic viticulture are quite odd. It is no wonder scepticism surrounds practices of burying cow horns full of manure in the soil during the autumn equinox and spraying ground quartz over vines. But these methods are beginning to gain a strong reputation on the competitive playing field of international wine because of genuine success, especially in France. There have been a number of very high-profile commercial converts in recent years, including Domaine Leroy in Burgundy, Château de la Roche-aux-Moines in the Loire, Maison Chapoutier in the Rhone Valley, and Domaine Zind Humbrecht in Alsace.

Pocket fact 🍷

In a recent blind testing conducted by Fortune *magazine, 10 biodynamic wines were judged against 10 conventionally made wines by leading industry experts, including a Master of Wine. The biodynamic wines were favoured nine out of the 10 times because they were deemed superior in flavour, aroma and texture. These results are subjective, but point to a bright future for biodynamic production.*

2

VARIETIES OF GRAPE

⊷ WHITE ⊶

Albariño
(Al-bar-een-yoh)

- Mostly grown in north-west Spain and Portugal
- Produces dry, refreshing, high-quality wines
- Characteristic flavours of apricot, lime and grapefruit always discernible, but more intense in the Spanish varieties

Chardonnay
(Shar-doh-nay)

- Classic white grape, first grown in Burgundy and Champagne, now all over the world
- A principal variety in the Champagne blend
- The only grape used to make Chablis and White Burgundy
- Old World Chardonnay is characterised by classic fruit flavours such as lemon and lime, whereas that from the New World exhibits more tropical fruit flavours and aromas
- Fermentation and aging in oak barrels lends lovely vanilla overtones to the wine

Chenin Blanc
(Shen-in blahnk)

- Originally grown in the Loire Valley, and more recently proved extremely successful in South America
- Clean on the tongue with notes of honey, vanilla, lime, guava and melon depending on style

(continued)

- Wines range in style from dry to very sweet
- In older wines, a mellow, nutty quality is distinguishable
- Most notable wine from this grape is Vouvray

Colombard
Call-om-bar

- Popular in New World countries such as California, South America and Australia because of its ability to produce a decent yield in high temperatures
- Creates reliable everyday wines that are fruity and crisp with occasional tropical highlights

Gewürztraminer
(Geh-vertz-trah-mee-ner)

- Grown most successfully in France, Germany and New Zealand as this grape prefers cooler climates
- Notable for its distinctive, pungent fragrance of roses, lychees and spice, with flavours of peach and apricot
- Can range from dry to sweet in style

Marsanne
(Mar-sarn)

- Grown almost exclusively in the northern Rhône valley
- Creates medium dry, full-bodied wines that have a rich flavour with pear, peach and spicy notes
- Commonly blended with Rousanne, and occasionally Viognier, to create more balanced wines

Muscat
(Moos-caht)

- Muscat refers to a family of over 200 grapes
- Two common types are Muscat Blanc à Petits Grains, which produces small grapes and is the highest quality, and Muscat d'Alexandre, which is a higher yielding vine
- It produces a remarkable range of wines from the very dry to the very sweet
- The juice is naturally high in sugar, so this is a variety favoured for use in semi-sweet or dessert wines
- An easy variety to detect as it has a unique, musky aroma with honey and marmalade flavours

Müller-Thurgau
(Moo-lerr turk cow)

- Aromatic, high yielding variety which is usually dry to off-dry
- Produces wine of note in Germany and Alsace

Muscadelle
(Moos-cah-dell)

- Part of the Muscat family
- One of the three approved varieties (alongside Sauvignon Blanc and Sémillon) for making white wines in the Sauternes region of France

Pinot Blanc
(Pee-no blahnk)

- Grown in Alsace, California, Italy, Germany and Austria
- Produces dry wines that are not dissimilar to Chardonnay in their light, pleasant qualities
- Grapes from the Alsace region are also used to produce aperitif wines notable for their creamy, apple flavour

Pinot Gris (Pinot Grigio)
(Pee-no gree or Pee-no gree-jo)

- Grown in France, Germany and Italy
- The region of Alsace creates deep coloured wines with rich and spicy aromas
- Varieties produced elsewhere create medium-bodied, well balanced wines with flavours that can range from citrus fruits through to apples and peaches
- Wines from this grape have a distinctive aroma of lily and honey blossom, and are pleasingly fresh in nature

Riesling
(Rees-ling)

- Grows best in cooler climates so popular in northern Europe, Germany in particular
- Recent years have seen cultivation further across the globe, resulting in a wider range of flavours and characteristics appearing within this previously very traditional grape variety
- Generally speaking, wines from this grape have a high acidity, but this is softened and complemented by delicate lime and apple flavours

(continued)

- Has a pleasing aroma of peach and honeysuckle, which can develop into a petrol nose as it ages
- Wines range in style from very dry to very sweet
- Some of the finest sweet wines in the world are a result of the effect of *Botrytis cinerea* on the grape, which creates a fabulous, rare and long-lasting wine

Rousanne (Roo-sarn)	• Mostly grown in the Rhône valley • Prized for its aromatic qualities and apricot flavour • Used in Hermitage Blanc, and often blended with Marsanne or Viognier
Sauvignon Blanc (Sew-veen-yon blahnk)	• Originally grown in the Loire valley and Bordeaux regions, it is now grown widely in New World countries, as it has the ability to tolerate heat better than many other varieties • Seems to have the ability to produce wines of distinction no matter where it is grown • Has a subtle nose of cut grass, gooseberry and melon, giving a fruity, exotic aroma • The delicacy of the grape means that it is easily overpowered and so is rarely aged in oak • Designed to be drunk young; most versions should be consumed within one year of harvesting • The grape behind two of the world's finest dry white wine styles, Sancerre and Pouilly-Fumé
Sémillon (Say-me-yon)	• A hardy variety that ripens earlier in the season than most grapes • Produces a wine with fairly high acidity, this variety is often blended with other grapes such as Sauvignon Blanc and Chardonnay to balance their tendency towards slightly sticky sweetness and create a fresh, zesty wine

	<ul><li>Creates young wines with citrus flavours of lemon and lime, but older wines mature to become full flavoured, rich and aromatic</li><li>Well suited to oak aging</li></ul>
Torrontés (Tor-ron-taze)	<ul><li>The principal white grape of Argentina</li><li>Creates quaffable, medium-bodied wines that are fresh, fruity and delicious</li></ul>
Ugni Blanc (Oo-nee blahnk)	<ul><li>Widely grown in France and Italy</li><li>The predominant grape of Cognac, and also the base of several Italian white wines</li><li>Creates medium-bodied wines with a certain zing, that can have a distinctive aroma of banana</li></ul>
Viognier Vee-on-yee-ay	<ul><li>Once grown only in the Rhône valley, this variety is now gaining popularity in California and Australia</li><li>Creates wines that can range from exquisite to very ordinary, depending on the producer</li><li>Wines mainly characterised by full bodied, fruity peach and apricot aromas that mingle with undertones of gentle spice, and a lovely golden colour</li></ul>

(continued)

⊷ RED ⊶

Baga
(Bah-guh)

- Almost exclusively planted in Portugal
- Grapes are incredibly thick skinned, resulting in wines that are high in tannin and acid
- The variety is susceptible to rot so is harvested early, resulting in the exacerbation of the already astringent quality of the wine produced
- Commonly used in Mateus rosé wine, where reduced tannins create a refreshing and pleasingly dry drink

Cabernet Franc
(Cab-er-nay frahnk)

- One of the six approved grapes for use in the blend of Bordeaux wines
- Creates light and sweet wines with good acidity, which means it adds life, freshness and well-rounded flavours to a Bordeaux blend, as well as a rich colour

Cabernet Sauvignon
(Cab-er-nay sew-veen-yon)

- The dominant variety in Bordeaux blends
- Grown in every major wine region of the world in the hope of creating a wine that can rival the eminent Bordeaux styles
- Produces wine that is deep in colour with plenty of tannin and a full body
- Aromas of blackcurrant, cherry, cedar and tobacco mingle and play on the senses, creating the complex flavour that is its prized blending quality
- Commonly aged in oak barrels for five to 10 years, which adds a woody, vanilla dimension to the wine

Carmenère
(Car-men-yerr)

- Almost exclusively grown in southern Chile
- Low tannin levels create a wine that is light and easy to drink, whose flavours benefit from tantalisingly rich fruit and spice qualities

Gamay
(Gam-ay)

- The grape of Beaujolais
- Distinctive in its deep violet colour and fruity aroma of strawberry and cherry

	• High acidity but low tannin levels create a fresh, light, unpretentious wine
	• Best drunk young (within two years of bottling)
Grenache (Garnacha) (Gre-na-sh)	• Found in numerous wine blends from around the world
	• Produces wines that are light in tannin and colour, and as such lends itself as a good variety for rosé (particularly popular in California)
	• Notable wines of this grape are the red Lirac and rosé Tavel, produced in the Rhône valley
Malbec (Mahl-bek)	• One of the six that can be used in the Bordeaux blend
	• A spicy variety with rich plum and black cherry flavour
	• Because of its strength, it is used sparingly in blends to add depth and length
	• Has become the flagship grape of Argentina
Merlot (Mare-low)	• One of the six that can be used in the Bordeaux blend
	• It is susceptible to fungal infections and can prove tricky to grow, so the quality of wines depend greatly on both location and skill of production
	• Characterised by plummy, berry flavours with the occasional chocolate undertone, a sweet and fruity bouquet, and a smooth, velvety quality
	• Commonly blended with other varieties, such as Cabernet Sauvignon, to soften the wine
Mourvèdre (More-veh-druh)	• A late ripening grape that performs best in warm climates, and so is predominantly planted along the Mediterranean coasts of France and Spain
	• Creates medium-bodied, deeply coloured wines that are full of cherry and berry flavours and distinctive for their gamy aroma
	• Used in the Rhône valley in blends of Cotes du Rhône and Châteauneuf du Pape
Nebbiolo (Neh-bee-oh-low)	• Can improve on aging for up to 10 years
	• Almost exclusively grown in Italy, it enjoys success in the Piedmont region where Barbaresco and Barolo are produced

(continued)

- Wines are full flavoured with a fruity, spicy flavour
- Can age very well

Petit Verdot (Peu-tea ver-doe)	• Another member of the Bordeaux Six • Gaining popularity in California as a minority blend to add depth and colour to wine • Produces a deep wine with a strong tannin structure and intense blackcurrant and damson flavours • Because of its tannic strength and depth of flavour, it is blended in as little as 1% to Bordeaux reds to add just a dash of these qualities to the final wine
Pinotage (Pee-no-tahje)	• A South African hybrid variety • Has a very individual aroma of smoky wood, plum and blackberry, with a kick of peppery spice • Pleasantly smooth to drink
Pinot Meunier (Pee-no mu-nee-ay)	• One of only three authorised grapes to be used in the Champagne blend (alongside Chardonnay and Pinot Noir) • A mutation of Pinot Noir but in use since the 16th century • Makes a fairly tart, acerbic wine that lends a bright and fresh edge to Champagne
Pinot Noir **(Spätburgunder)** (Pee-no nwahr)	• The red grape of Burgundy • Also used to add body and richness to Champagne • Notoriously difficult to grow as it flourishes in a climate with warm days and cool nights • Produced and popular worldwide • As a rule, it is light in colour and low in tannin, with notable cherry and strawberry aromas and flavours • Can be aged for three to 12 years depending on its quality
Sangiovese **(Brunello)** (San-joe-va-say)	• The primary grape used in northern Italy • Produces Tuscan Chianti and Brunello di Montalicino

	• Also being grown in California and Australia where they are experimenting with blending
	• Produces fruity, lively, medium-bodied wines with good acidity that adds a racey edge to an otherwise smooth drinking experience
Syrah (Shiraz) (See-rah)	• In the Rhône it produces full-bodied, inky coloured wines that are characterised by spicy aromas
	• When grown in the warmer climate of Australia, wines are sweeter, riper and almost jammy in flavour, but retain the distinctive spicy quality
Tempranillo (Tinto del Pais, Tinto Roriz) (Tem-pra-nee-oh)	• Grown on the Iberian peninsula of Spain and Portugal
	• The major grape in Rioja
	• Creates medium-bodied, acidic wines that have a rich colour and flavours of blackcurrant and plum
	• Often blended with Cabernet Sauvignon or Grenache
	• Benefits from oak aging, which adds vanilla softness and a smoky complexity to the wine
Tinto Cão (Tin-toe Kai-oe)	• Grown in small quantities in Portugal only
	• Historically used for port, recent experimentation proves that it can yield excellent table wines which have floral aromas, fresh flavours and a captivatingly harmonious palate
	• Wines are best for aging
Touriga Nacional (Too-ree-gah nas-see-o-nahl)	• A Portuguese variety that is *the* grape for port
	• Creates deep coloured, tannic wines with concentrated flavours that are very dry in the mouth
	• More recently being used to create red table wine as well as port
Zinfandel (Zin-fan-dell)	• Grown almost exclusively in California
	• Produces heavyweight reds with intense flavours of blackberry and spice
	• Produces a fruity, off-dry rosé known as white Zinfandel

3

WINE REGIONS OF THE WORLD

Understanding the nuances of wine production can seem daunting, but it basically relies on an understanding of exactly what is made exactly where. In this long chapter, we'll look at the major wine producing countries of the globe.

Top 10 world wine producers

1. France	5.35 million tonnes
2. Italy	4.71 million tonnes
3. Spain	3.64 million tonnes
4. USA	2.23 million tonnes
5. Argentina	1.54 million tonnes
6. Australia	1.41 million tonnes
7. China	1.40 million tonnes
8. South Africa	1.01 million tonnes
9. Chile	0.97 million tonnes
10. Germany	0.89 million tonnes

~~~┥ ARGENTINA ┝~~~

HISTORY

Argentina is a country whose colourful cultural influences are matched only by its rich diversity of grape varieties. Most of these varieties were brought over in a wave of immigration from Spain and Italy during the mid-19th century. Argentina is a country which produces a great volume of wine, although mostly low-quality plonk to satisfy the home market.

It was not until the mid 1990s that Argentina began to dip its toes in the international wine market, when a rise in economic wealth allowed for greater investment in the industry. 'Flying wine-makers' have begun to improve quality, with increased investment from Old World wine companies leading an attempt to market Argentine wines internationally.

Pocket fact 🍷

Argentina is now the world's fifth largest wine producer, although only 10% is exported – a whopping 90% is consumed in the country itself.

CLIMATE AND GEOGRAPHY

Argentina is a mixture of extreme landscapes, yielding a great diversity of wines. The main secret of Argentine grape-growing success is the altitude of its vineyards.

The lowest vineyards are situated at altitudes of around 900m above sea level. This would be unthinkable to European viticul-turalists, but it is this height that creates the temperatures that allow Argentine grapes to flourish.

Overnight, temperatures on this high ground drop to levels low enough to encourage red grapes to develop good flavours and deep colours. In the northern vineyards, temperatures are several degrees lower as standard, which allows for the growth of white grapes that produce wines with sumptuous aromas.

GRAPE VARIETIES

Argentina is home to a wealth of different wine grape varieties, and a few of the most notable are listed here.

Red

- Malbec is the signature grape of Argentina and produces its optimum flavours when grown on these soils. Creates a smoky, spicy wine that can be punctuated with jammy fruit flavours.

- Other varieties include Cabernet Sauvignon, Bonarda, Merlot, Pinot Noir, Sangiovese, Syrah and Tempranillo.

White

- Torrontés is the grape that features most strongly on the international market for Argentina. It makes an easy-drinking, medium-bodied wine with floral and herbal fragrances that give way to crisp, fresh, fruity flavours.

- Also grown widely are Chardonnay, Chenin Blanc, Sauvignon Blanc, Sémillon, Riesling and Ugni Blanc.

KEY WINE PRODUCING AREAS

Argentine wines fall under similar rules of appellation to that on the continent: wines are labelled by region and vineyard. Some 90% of Argentine wine comes from the Cuyo region north of Santiago, encompassing San Juan and Mendoza, although there are other notable areas worth exploring.

Salta

- The northernmost wine-growing region of Argentina, and home to the world's highest vineyards.

- Grapes grown include Cabernet Sauvignon, Malbec, Syrah and Chardonnay, but Torrontés is the signature grape of the region.

- Look out for Torrontés wines from the *Cafayete region*.

La Rioja

- Wine varieties include Malbec, Syrah, Bonarda, Cabernet Sauvignon and Torrontés.

- Best known for its Torrontés Riojana, which is produced by the local wine cooperative.

San Juan

- The region's landscape with its numerous valleys provides ideal conditions for a number of grape varieties. Because of this, almost a quarter of all Argentine wines come from this area.

- Varieties include Moscatel, Malbec, Cabernet Sauvignon, Merlot, Bonarda, Chardonnay, Sauvignon Blanc, Viognier, Torrontés and Syrah.

- Famed for its sweet *Moscatel de Alexandria*, San Juan is also gaining international repute for its fine Syrah wines.

Mendoza

Classed as one of the world's eight Great Wine Capitals and divided into the following sub-regions:

Luján de Cuyo	This area is well known for producing quality wines from the Malbec grape. Vineyards of note are *Vistalba, Perdriel, Agrelo* and *Las Compuertas*.
San Rafael	This southern area was the first in Argentina to qualify for its own appellation. This area is the main producer of Chenin, but other varieties such as Chardonnay, Sauvignon Blanc, Malbec, Merlot and Cabernet Sauvignon are also cultivated.
Uco Valley	The most distinguished region of wine production, notable for creating the finest wines in the country.
Central Mendoza	Not an area that produces the most exciting wines, but does create very pleasant table wines.
Tupungato	This sub-region produces the finest Argentine Chardonnays.

Patagonia

- Production is centred in the high altitude valley of San Patricio del Chanar where there are plantations of Cabernet Sauvignon, Malbec, Pinot Noir, Chardonnay and Sauvignon Blanc.

- Growers claim it to be the southernmost vineyards on Earth (but Kiwi growers are potentially a little further south).

- Good producers include: *Bodegas del Fin del Mundo* and *Bodegas Familia Schroeder.*

One to watch: Bodega Familia Zuccardi 🍇

This family-owned estate produces an excellent range and is moving towards entirely organic production. Its Malbec is an excellent example of Argentina's signature grape.

Pocket fact 🍷

The eight wine Capitals of the World are linked together by an organisation intended to promote their economic growth. The eight are:

- Bordeaux (France)
- Bilbao (Rioja) (Spain)
- Mendoza (Argentina)
- Cape Town (South Africa)
- Firenze (Italy)
- Mainz (Rheinhessen) (Germany)
- Porto (Portugal)
- San Francisco (Napa Valley) (USA)

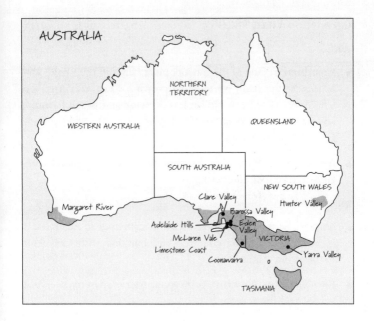

AUSTRALIA

NORTHERN TERRITORY

WESTERN AUSTRALIA

QUEENSLAND

SOUTH AUSTRALIA

NEW SOUTH WALES

Margaret River

Clare Valley

Hunter Valley

Barossa Valley

Adelaide Hills

Eden Valley

McLaren Vale

VICTORIA

Limestone Coast

Coonawarra

Yarra Valley

TASMANIA

~~| AUSTRALIA |~~

HISTORY

In the past 10 years, the Australian wine industry has boomed and it is now one of the leading exporters in the world. A combination of tax incentives, growing confidence from continuously high sales, and investment from overseas winemakers has put Australia at the top of the wine production hierarchy.

GRAPE VARIETIES

White

- Chardonnay: One of the most popular wines in the world, and as such is the main white grape grown for export. Australian Chardonnays tend to exhibit lovely melon and peach flavours, and are often aged in oak for a year or so to enhance their smooth vanilla flavour.

- Also produces Pinot Gris, Riesling, Sémillon, Sauvignon Blanc, Gewürztraminer and Verdelho.

Red

- Shiraz: The most famous red wine to come out of Australia, it is full bodied, richly coloured and bursting with rich fruit flavours and a hint of spice.

- Also produces Cabernet Sauvignon, Merlot, Grenache, Petit Verdot and Pinot Noir.

KEY WINE PRODUCING AREAS

Western Australia

Although this region produces less than 5% of the country's output, the wines rank amongst the highest in terms of quality. They retain a lightness which distinguishes them from traditional Aussie 'fruit bombs'.

Margaret River

The most notable area for winemaking within this region, it enjoys lush vegetation and a climate that is far more conducive to grape cultivation than anywhere else in the country.

Its reputation has been built on its Cabernet Sauvignon. Some excellent Shiraz, Chardonnay and Sauvignon Blanc also make this an exciting wine region.

One to watch: Howard Park 🍇

Howard Park produces an excellent oaked Chardonnay with nutty complexity on the nose alongside a zesty fruit palate. Its Shiraz shows ripe black fruit alongside a chocolatey finish accentuated by the fresh mint and herbs on the nose. In the Cabernet Sauvignon, vanilla and blackcurrant accentuate the spicy, muscular feel of this superb wine.

South Australia

This is the winemaking hub of Australia. It produces an ever-increasing majority of vintages and is home to all of the important wine research organisations. Within this region, there are seven key areas:

Barossa Valley

- This area is absolutely saturated with vines, as it is Australia's biggest quality wine district.
- Shiraz is the grape from which the most distinctive wines are produced in the region. Under the blistering sun, the Shiraz grapes seem to reach their full ripening potential to produce potent, spicy wines with rich, chocolatey flavours.
- If you are looking for good independent producers, *Peter Lehmann* and *Hewitson* are great bets.

Eden Valley

- This area only recently gained distinction from the Barossa Valley, thanks to family wine company *Yalumba of Angaston,* which began to mark it out as Riesling country in the 1960s. Rieslings grown high in the hills of the Eden Valley are remarkable for their beautiful floral and mineral aromas.

Clare Valley

- Famed for Riesling, Cabernet Sauvignon and Shiraz, the vineyards are at a fairly high altitude, creating the cool nights that are good at preserving the acidity levels in these grapes.

- Unlike other areas of South Australia, few producers in Clare Valley have associations with large corporations (the exceptions being *Leasingham,* which is owned by *Hardy's*, and *Annie's Lane,* which is owned by *Fosters*).

- For Australia's finest examples of Riesling, look to *Jeffrey Grosset*, *Kilkaroon* and *TK Wines*. For Cabernet Sauvignon and Shiraz, *Jeffrey Grosset* is again very good, as are *Wendouree* and *Jim Barry*.

McLaren Vale

- McLaren Vale has a long history in Australian wine production, and is still home to distinguished wine firm *Hardy's* and the famous *Amery* vineyards.

- Some good Grenache comes from the vineyards of Blewitt Springs, whilst Kangarilla produces excellent Shiraz. Cabernet Sauvignon and Merlot are also delicious, and wineries to look out for include *Geoff Merrill*, *Tatachilla*, *Chapel Hill* and *Woodstock*.

Adelaide Hills

- The Mount Lofty ranges in the Adelaide Hills are usually overshadowed by cloud, which maintains the continuously cool temperatures necessary to produce the zesty Sauvignon Blanc, bursting with the citrus flavours that this area is known for.

- The vineyards of Gumeracha, more southerly than Mount Lofty, are warmer and ideal for growing beautifully ripe Cabernet Sauvignon. In a similar geographical area, Mount Barker produces masterful Shiraz. Pinot Noir and Merlot, though less widely grown, can also produce high-quality wines.

Sparkling wines are also a feature. Those from producers *Nepenthe* and *Starve Dog Lane* are worth trying.

Limestone Coast

- As the name suggests, this area has loamy soils that encourage vine cultivation. Couple this with a warm climate and the conditions are good for some successful winemaking. Grapes grown include Riesling, Chardonnay, Cabernet Sauvignon, Shiraz and Pinot Noir.
- The majority of the grapes harvested in the area go into blends, but those that do not make easy-drinking wines that are fairly uncomplicated.

Coonawarra

- The soil of Coonawarra is quite remarkable, being vibrant red in colour. Below this bright, crumbly topsoil is a layer of free-draining limescale, and below that again fresh water. This combination makes for the perfect growing terrain.
- Signature wines of the region are an easy-drinking Shiraz and the juicy Cabernet Sauvignon. Top producers include *Katnook*, *Majella* and *Wynns*.

One to watch: Knappstein 🍇

A small producer of excellent quality wines in the Clare Valley region. Look out for their Riesling with a delightfully lime and citrus nose that leads into clean, lush fruit on the palate.

Victoria

The smallest state on the Australian mainland, Victoria is nonetheless important to the country's wine economy, not least due to its diverse vine growing conditions that range from the arid inland areas to the cool Macedon Ranges nearer the south coast.

Muscat is the wine to try. It is produced in the incredibly hot north-eastern area of the state where the wines thrive under the relentless heat of the sun. Muscat from this region can be singularly rich and sweet, with flavours of caramel and raisin.

One to watch: Giaconda 🍇

Giaconda's Chardonnay is fascinatingly complex, with a nutty, honeyed nose followed by a sensuous palate with savoury notes balanced by good acidity. Its Pinot Noir shows excellent forest fruit notes on the nose whilst the palate expands into fleshy plum flavours hemmed in by subtle oak.

Yarra Valley

Although Pinot Noir and Chardonnay from the Yarra Valley are a popular choice, its name should be synonymous with the finest sparkling wine Australia has to offer. It is also the oldest wine-growing region in Australia, dating back to 1837. A cool, maritime climate ensures that its sparkling whites possess excellent acidity.

In 1986, *Moët & Chandon* established the *Domaine Chandon* here, and the area continues to produce high-quality *méthode traditionnelle* sparkling wine. *Dromana Estates* is another excellent producer, experimenting successfully with many Italian varieties to produce spicy, intense Nebbiolo and beautifully yeasty yet zippy Arneis.

One to watch: De Bortoli 🍇

Popular for its full bodied Chardonnay, which shows rich aromatic fruit balanced against excellent mineral note, De Bortoli also produces excellent Cabernet Sauvignon which is pleasantly dark in its flavours whilst being incredibly smooth.

Hunter Valley

The Hunter Valley is split into upper and lower sections, with Sémillon predominating in the cooler lower valley and Chardonnay in the drip-irrigated and warmer upper valley. The two sections are split by the Hunter river, with Sydney a mere 160km further south.

Hunter Valley wine has become extremely popular in the UK, with some of the larger producers very well stocked in UK wine stores. Prominent producers include *Tyrell's*, *Lindemans* and *McGuigan's*. Reds from the Hunter Valley can exhibit a characteristic savoury note which likens them to Italian reds. Hunter Valley Sémillons tend towards a beautiful, buttery smoothness, and have garnered praise for well-aged releases.

One to watch: Brokenwood 🍇

Brokenwood's powerful Shiraz is an excellent example of the peppery ripeness it can deliver. It has an impressive range of different price level bottles but its top release — the Graveyard Vineyard — is beautifully rich and complex, and a stunning wine.

Tasmania

With a cooler climate than much of Australia, the island of Tasmania is a relative newcomer to the wine industry. It now produces some excellent cool-weather varieties, with zippy, gooseberry tinted Sauvignon Blancs, oaky yet refreshingly honeyed Chardonnays and supple, suave Burgundy-style Pinot Noirs.

One to watch: Tamar Ridge 🍇

An excellent producer led by Dr Andrew Pirie, the man behind the Tasmanian wine revival, Tamar Ridge's Sauvignon Blanc is zippy with Kiwi-style gooseberry notes. Its Pinot Noir is a star, with ripe cherry flavours which beguile amidst a delicately smooth texture.

Pocket fact 🍷

Australians are credited with having invented both boxed wine and screw-top closures.

⊣ AUSTRIA ⊢

Notable mainly for its production of the white grape *Grüner Veltliner*, Austria is a fairly small exporter. Nevertheless, the increasingly popular *Grüner Veltliner* is characterised by dryness and notes of white pepper as well as balanced acidity. It is an excellent food wine, matching often difficult foods such as artichokes and asparagus. Excellent producers include *Schloss Gobelsburg* and *Weingut Prager*.

⊣ BULGARIA ⊢

This is the biggest exporter amongst the former Soviet countries. The best Bulgarian wines are labelled *Controliran*, which is their AC equivalent and a step up from Declared Geographic Origin (DGO). The wine-growing regions can be divided into three regions – eastern, northern and southern. The east comprises of the Black Sea coastline, where the *Novi Pazar* DGO region produces excellent Chardonnays. In the north, the slopes of the Balkan mountains provide excellent sun for a variety of noble reds. Perhaps the most famous of these is the Cabernet Sauvignon from *Svischistov*. The south is the most productive region, with *Stambolovo* and *Sakar* important regions for quality Merlot production.

⤙ CANADA ⤚

The extreme cold of the Canadian winters makes it the perfect place for the production of Ice Wine, for which Canada has been lauded at various international competitions. Made from frozen grapes, this dessert wine is gloriously sweet, retaining a naturally high acidity that makes it somewhat clean tasting. For excellent Ice Wine, try award-winning producers *Vidal* and *Henry of Pelham*.

There are also genuinely good Bordeaux blends and Syrahs being produced in Ontario by wineries such as *Daniel Lenko*. Whilst most wine production takes place around Lake Ontario, the Okanagan valley some way west in British Columbia is home to excellent producers such as *Sumac Ridge* and *Wild Goose*.

One to watch: Inniskillin 🍇

Famous for its delectable award-winning Ice Wines, try some of Inniskillen's Bordeaux blend reds, which show off the excellent potential of the Okanagan valley as a wine region.

ⵗ CHILE ⵗ

HISTORY

Wine has been produced in Chile for hundreds of years, having been introduced by conquistadors in the 15th century. But it wasn't until the 1990s that Chile gained international recognition as a producer of fine wines. During this decade, a combination of a more democratic and commercially minded political atmosphere and a streamlined focus on producing quality wines helped to propel Chile to the forefront of the global winemaking industry.

CLIMATE AND GEOGRAPHY

Chile has a quite extraordinary diversity of climate and geography, encased as it is between a huge coastline to the west, the Atacama desert in the north and the ice-fields of Patagonia in the south. Because of these natural limitations, the potential winemaking regions are restricted to a fairly small central area of the country that enjoys a more temperate, Mediterranean-style climate.

GRAPE VARIETIES

The reliably warm climate of central Chile is ideal for growing almost any variety of grape. The most popular varieties that are cultivated across Chile are described below.

Red

- Merlot is the star variety of Chile, and wines from this grape rank as some of the best in the world. The traditional rich plummy flavours and unique smoothness are captured in Chilean Merlots, with the addition of a distinctive peppery edge that is particularly pleasing.

- Carmenère is a variety that is grown almost solely in Chile. It produces easy-drinking, medium bodied red wines that have lovely fruit flavours and spicy highlights. Imagine a Merlot with greater weight.

- Other grapes grown include Cabernet Sauvignon, Syrah and Pinot Noir.

White

- Commonly grown grapes include Sauvignon Blanc, Chardonnay, Riesling and Gewürztraminer.

- Generally, whites produced in the warmer climate of Chile have the additional flavours of tropical fruits such as lychees and passionfruit, which their European counterparts tend to lack.

Pocket fact 🍷

Carmenère is often referred to as 'the lost grape of Bordeaux'. It was wiped out when the Phylloxera *louse hit Europe, only to be taken to Chile when French winegrowers emigrated in search of better fortunes.*

KEY WINE PRODUCING AREAS

In 1995, Chile introduced a new quality control system. This insists that wines labelled as a certain grape variety have to contain at least 75% of that grape, and if they include a vintage on the label the wine must consist of at least 75% of grapes harvested in the year stated.

This new appellation system also created distinct wine regions.

Aconcagua Valley

- Located in northern Chile, this region is hot and arid, making it best suited to red wine production.

- Its tastiest reds come from Cabernet Sauvignon.

- Most significant wines come from the *Errázuriz* estate.

Casablanca Valley

- A cool and coastal region notable for producing quality white wines from Chardonnay and Sauvignon Blanc.

- Look out for the *Casa Lapostolle* wines produced by leading Chilean winemaker Ignacio Recabarren.

Maipó Valley

- One of the warmest of the wine-growing regions in central Chile.

- Mainly produces Cabernet Sauvignon of a high-quality.

- Big producers to look out for from this region are *Concha y Toro, Santa Rita* and *Santa Carolina*.

Rapel Valley

- As the largest of the wine regions, the Rapel Valley has a range of climatic and geographical variables so a variety of wines are produced.

- Merlot is notable; look out for producers such as *Carmen* and *Mont Gras*.

- Interesting Pinot Noir, Viognier and Gewürztraminer wines are produced by *Cono Sur*.

San Antonio Valley

- Situated in southern Chile, this region has a cooler climate that is moderated by the ocean.

- Sauvignon Blanc and Chardonnay are grown successfully, as are Pinot Noir and Syrah.

- Primary producers include *Casa Marin, Matetic* and *Amayna*.

Curicó and Maule

- These areas combine high rainfall with plentiful sunshine.

- A good reputation is built primarily on its quality red wines, with Cabernet Sauvignon leading the field.

- Look for offerings from *San Pedro, Miguel Torres, Domaine Oriental, Montes* and *Valdevieso*.

Southern Chile

- The most southern wine region of Chile encompasses the sub-regions of Itata, Bío Bío and Malleco.

- A cool, fairly wet climate favours varieties of Riesling, Gewürztraminer, Sauvignon Blanc, Chardonnay and Pinot Noir.

- Good producers include *Viña Gracia*, *Viña Porta* and *Concha y Toro at Mulchén*.

One to watch: Santa Alicia Vineyards 🍇

This winery satisfies at all levels. Its Cabernet Sauvignons are rich and complex with dark fruits whilst the Malbec (an innovative variety for a Chilean winery) shows good cherry and blackcurrant fruits alongside a firm tannic body.

⊶ CHINA ⊷

Chinese wine is not commonly seen in Europe. Regulation is lax and Chinese grape wine can sometimes be blended with imported grape juice of unstated origin. Low-end wines are largely produced for the home market and show little promise.

This is not to say that there is no quality wine production in China, however, and this can be found amongst higher-end producers. *Changyu* is the oldest winery in China, dating back to 1892, and produces wines from noble varieties such as Cabernet Sauvignon. Likewise the *China Silk* winery has produced award-winning wines which are now exported to the USA.

⊶ ENGLAND ⊷

Grapes have been grown in England since the Romans decamped here, although quality has been challenged by an unpromising climate. A shift from Burgundian practices to more Germanic inspired winemaking has seen some vineyards in England flourish.

There are five grapes recommended for making quality wine in England:

- Müller-Thurgau: Less popular due to vine disease, an aromatic grape
- Huxelrebe: Often used for dessert wine – a grapey, intense palate
- Madeleine-Angevine: Low in acidity and high-yielding
- Reichsteiner: High sugar content and reliable yield
- Schönburger: Low acidity with a spicy quality

Increasingly sparkling wine is predominating. Made in the traditional Champagne method, some English growers are now sticking to Chardonnay, Pinot Meunier and Pinot Noir to improve quality.

One to watch: Nyetimber 🍇

Investment into its wineries has also proven commercially successful, and Nyetimber is probably the best English producer, with its sparkling whites comparing favourably to some Champagnes in blind tastings.

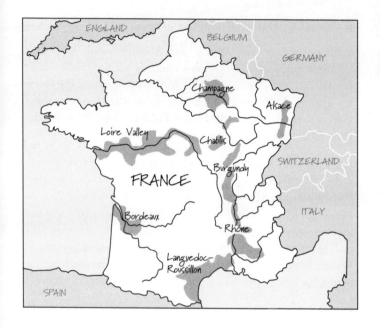

⤙ FRANCE ⤚

'Burgundy for kings, Champagne for duchesses, claret for gentlemen.'
French proverb

HISTORY

Since the Roman times, France has been established as the greatest wine producing nation in the world. The outstanding cultivation of well-known Cabernet Sauvignon, Chardonnay, Pinot Noir and Merlot grapes to name but a few, in the renowned and respected great wine regions of Burgundy, Bordeaux and Champagne have sealed its name at the forefront of the history of wine.

CLIMATE AND GEOGRAPHY

With borders on the Atlantic and Mediterranean, as well as Germany and Spain, France has a uniquely balanced influence of coastal and intercontinental influences washing across the country. This results in a huge diversity of climates and landscapes that hold between them enormous potential for numerous grape varieties to flourish in each differing terrain.

KEY WINE PRODUCING AREAS

Burgundy

Famed for its powerful yet refined reds (typically Pinot Noir) and its distinctively mineral-rich whites (typically Chardonnay), it is one of the largest and therefore most complicated regions of France. It's best to understand the labelling for the entire region before we look at the virtues of specific areas.

Côte d'Or

The Côte d'Or is undeniably the richest and most important of the wine regions of Burgundy. Geographically, it lies along an ancient geological fault line that has dredged calcium and nutrient-rich deposits from the seabed onto the surface. Over time this has created an undulating mountainous landscape with fertile soils that are ideal for the cultivation of vines at various altitudes.

Within the Côte d'Or region itself, are two further sub-regions.

Côte de Beaune

This area lies in the southern part of the Côte d'Or, and encompasses wines made both in Beaune and the surrounding villages.

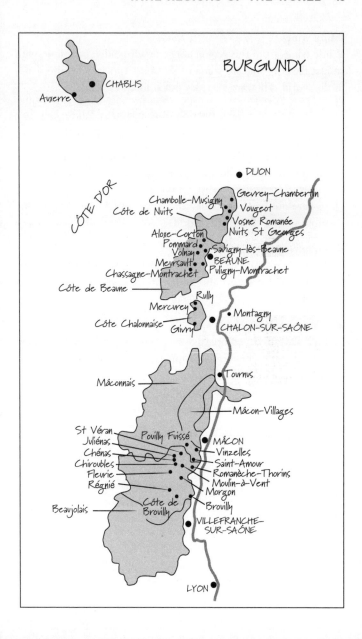

BURGUNDY

CHABLIS

Auxerre

CÔTE D'OR

DIJON

Chambolle-Musigny
Côte de Nuits
Gevrey-Chambertin
Vougeot
Vosne Romanée
Nuits St Georges

Aloxe-Corton
Pommard
Volnay
Meursault
Chassagne-Montrachet
Savigny-lès-Beaune
BEAUNE
Puligny-Montrachet

Côte de Beaune

Rully

Mercurey
Côte Chalonnaise
Givry
Montagny
CHALON-SUR-SAÔNE

Mâconnais

Tournus

Mâcon-Villages

St Véran
Juliénas
Chénas
Chiroubles
Fleurie
Régnié

Pouilly Fuissé

MÂCON
Vinzelles
Saint-Amour
Romanèche-Thorins
Moulin-à-Vent
Morgon

Beaujolais

Côte de
Brouilly
Brouilly

VILLEFRANCHE-
SUR-SAÔNE

LYON

White wines
White wines from this region are generally golden in colour, with robust flavours and are some of the most expensive white wines in the world. They are very dry but smooth to drink.

Look out for wines from the following villages:

- **Meursault**
  The heartland of White Burgundy, the soil lends itself to the cultivation of Chardonnay grapes and as such this village produces whites of great distinction. Wines are buttery and rich in hazelnut and vanilla flavours, and as such are some of the most sought after in the world.

- **Puligny-Montrachet**
  Rich, deep white wines with a mineral quality that provides a steely, solid core around which more complex flavours can develop.

- **Chassagne-Montrachet**
  Full flavoured, complex wines with densely concentrated fruit flavours of lemon and apple, accompanied by a pinch of spice.

> *Pocket tip* ♆
> *Wines from lesser known villages in the Côte de Beaune region, such as St Romain, St Aubin, Santenay and Auxey-Duresses also produce some lovely white wines that are more reasonably priced than those coming from the top three villages.*

Red wines
Red wines from the Côte de Beaune are generally classed as slightly lighter than their counterparts in the more northern Côte de Nuits area of the Côte d'Or region. But this is a

loose generalisation at best, and reds can vary from medium-bodied, fruity wines through to complex and deep drinking experiences.

Look out for wines from the following villages and their vineyards:

- **Aloxe-Corton**
  Reds from this area are characteristically silky with hints of exotic spices.

- **Beaune**
  The vineyards of Beaune are primarily dedicated to the growth of Pinot Noir, and produce wines that are rich in body, with earthy, meaty flavours broken up by tones of red fruit.

- **Savigny-lès-Beaune**
  Again, vineyards of this area are mostly red, and wines are powerful, intense and rich.

- **Pommard**
  These wines are best when they are mature, as they are muscular wines with a good depth of tannin and gamey aromas. They also have earthy, mineral tones, making them arguably the most intense of the red Burgundy wines.

- **Volnay**
  All wines from Volnay share a fantastic aroma that encompasses red berries, flowers and spice. They are the feminine foil to the masculine reds of Pommard.

Vintage chart: Côte de Beaune

Year	Rating	Year	Rating
2007	87	2002	90
2006	88	2001	78
2005	94	2000	80
2004	80	1999	93
2003	88	1998	82

(continued)

Vintage chart: Côte de Beaune (continued)

Year	Rating	Year	Rating
1997	90	1988	86
1996	91	1987	79
1995	87	1986	72
1994	73	1985	87
1993	81	1983	78
1992	82	1982	80
1991	72	1981	74
1990	90	1980	78
1989	88	1979	77

Côte de Nuits

Encompassing the northern area of the Côte d'Or region, the Côte de Nuits is renowned for its red wines, the most famous of which come from Pinot Noir grapes in the vineyards of these villages:

● *Vosne-Romanée*

This area is dedicated red wine country, creating Burgundy with strong, positive flavours that are a little rough with tannins when young but fantastic after prolonged aging.

The most sought after reds from this area come from the *Domaine de la Romanée-Conti* in the form of *La Romanée-Conti* and *La Tâche*. These wines are complex with subtle dark berry flavours and exotic spices, and produce velvety warmth in the mouth.

● *Gevery-Chambertin*

Produces the Burgundian reds that age best. These are weighty, full-bodied, complex wines that are unparalleled in their luxury.

● *Chambolle-Musigny*

A wine which embodies the red from the region is the *Grand Cru Musigny* in which delicate fruit aromas belie a powerful wine with expressive flavours.

- **Nuits-Saint-Georges**
  A productive and popular village that produces fine Burgundian reds that offer dependable excellence.

Vintage chart: Côte de Nuits

Year	Rating	Year	Rating
2007	88	1993	85
2006	88	1992	69
2005	98	1991	86
2004	85	1990	92
2003	93	1989	87
2002	93	1988	85
2001	84	1987	85
2000	85	1986	74
1999	91	1985	87
1998	83	1983	85
1997	92	1982	81
1996	90	1981	72
1995	90	1980	84
1994	72	1979	77

Côte Chalonnaise

This region is the home of both moderately priced generic *AC Bourgogne* and the *Premier Cru* areas of Rully, Mercurey, Givry and Montagny.

Mâconnais

A slightly warmer climate than the Côte d'Or allows this region to grow Chardonnay with great success. The grapes produce easy-drinking wines full of creamy fruit flavours and beautiful floral aromas. *AC Macon-Villages* covers the better dry whites, centred on a cluster of excellent villages, with *Pouilly-Fuissé* the top appellation in this region. Value can be had in *AC St Véran*, which produces an excellent white in the style of its more prestigious neighbours.

Beaujolais

The granite soils of Burgundy transform Gamay grapes into a red that is inimitably light, fresh and fruity. *Beaujolais* and *Beaujoiais-Nouveau* are the most quaffable but aim higher with something from the *cru* villages of which there are 10: Juliénas, Saint-Amour, Chénas, Moulin-à-Vent, Fleurie, Chiroubles, Morgon, Régnié, Brouilly, and Côte de Brouilly.

Pocket fact 🍷

The famous race to bring the first bottle of Beaujolais Nouveau back to Britain happens on the third Thursday of November every year.

Chablis

The cooler climate of this region, coupled with its cold limestone soils, produces Chardonnay that is dramatically different from that of any other area of the world. In good *Chablis*, the exuberant qualities typical of Chardonnay are replaced by dignified flavours of stone and minerals, with a hint of freshly cut grass. Look out for growing information on your label: 'Commune' means the flat vineyards surrounding villages; 'premier cru' denotes sloping hillside vineyards and 'grand cru' alludes to the best hillside vineyards.

Burgundy labelling

Burgundy labelling operates on a pyramid structure, with Grand Cru, the best quality, at the tip of the pyramid levelling down to regional appellations at the foot of the pyramid. These are listed with their percentage in the total output of Burgundy:

1) Grand Cru (1%)

The highest quality wines of the region, produced from the most auspiciously positioned vineyards. Only about 30 regions carry this distinguished classification. They all have their own appellation which takes the form of the name of the vineyard.

2) Premier Cru (11%)

Second only to the Grand Crus, although still produced from grapes grown in highly reputable vineyards. These wines take an appellation in the form of the village name and the name of the vineyard in which the grapes were grown.

3) Appellation Communale (23%)

Made with grapes from the more average vineyards. The label of these wines usually only includes the name of the village in which the vineyard is located. Increasingly the name of the vineyard is included, but in smaller print so as to distinguish them from the Premier Cru wines.

4) Bourgogne (65%)

The lowest ranking wines, these are produced from less propitiously sited vineyards and are only allowed to use the appellation Bourgogne on their labels.

One to watch: Albert Bichot 🍇

This merchant is responsible for domains producing some extremely fine Burgundian whites from both the Côte Chalonnaise and the Côte de Beaune regions. These wines demonstrate the finesse, elegance and strength of Burgundian Chardonnay.

Vintage chart: White Burgundy

Year	Rating	Year	Rating
2007	86	1993	72
2006	89	1992	90
2005	91	1991	70
2004	90	1990	87
2003	84	1989	92
2002	92	1988	82
2001	86	1987	80
2000	88	1986	90
1999	89	1985	89
1998	84	1983	86
1997	89	1982	88
1996	92	1981	86
1995	93	1980	75
1994	77	1979	88

Champagne

This is the only region of the winemaking world that is allowed to label its sparkling produce as *Champagne*, and such a mark of distinction allows its reputation to go from strength to strength (along with its sales figures). As early as 1665, demand was high in trade centres such as London for sparkling wine, and the 17th century saw the birth of many of the biggest Champagne houses as production evolved to meet these desires.

Dom Pérignon is the monk credited with the birth of the industry and, although many areas claim to have invented sparkling wine, Champagne is the only one which can claim to have made it a success. Specifically, the monk from the Abbey of Hautvilliers is seen as being the first to appreciate that this sparkling wine was better if it was blended across several varieties.

This blending practice has endured, and the majority of Champagne has been produced by large wineries that blended grapes from all over the region to produce their own distinctive wines (*Bollinger, Reims, Laurent-Perrier* and *Veuve-Cliquot* are all good examples).

More recently though, there has been an increase in smaller makers who use grapes from distinct areas within the region gaining international attention. These include producers *Jean Noël Haton, Louis Roederer* and *Billecart-Salmon*.

Only three grapes are distinguished enough to make it into the finest Champagne blends: Pinot Noir, Chardonnay and Pinot Meunier. Most Champagnes contain a varying proportion of these grapes. For more information on the processes by which Champagne is made, see p.8.

Champagnes are also labelled according to how dry or otherwise they are. These terms do overlap, allowing producers some scope in the marketing of their wines and meaning that the *Brut* of one house may be considered *Extra Sec* by another producer.

Brut Zéro/Brut Sauvage Ultra/Brut/Extra Brut	Bracingly Dry
Brut	Very Dry
Extra Sec	Dry
Sec	Off-dry
Demi-sec	Sweet
Doux	Luxuriantly sweet

Champagnes also differ widely in their blend of different vintages. There are several different classifications that control the *assemblage* (blending) of a Champagne.

- Vintage Champagnes are fuller and more intense in fruit, coming from named vintage of exceptionally high-quality.

- Non-Vintage Champagnes are blended from different vintages to produce a house style, and this constitutes the vast majority of production.

In some years premium Cuvées are declared, in which case Pinot Meunier is usually left out of this single Vintage blend. As they depend on a perfect harmony of weather factors, these Champagne releases are rare and resultantly expensive. Dom

Pérignon began blending his wine for the royal court and, in many ways, that is still where it resides today as one of the most consistent status symbols throughout the ages.

One to watch: Pierre Gimonnet 🍇

Outside the club of grand Champagne houses, there are some excellent individual producers of whom Gimonnet is pre-eminent. His releases are an excellent tonic to over-familiar brand names and some Vintage releases display exceptional elegance.

Bordeaux

The Bordeaux wine region lies within the Gironde *département* in the south-west of France at the confluence of the Garonne and Dordogne rivers. It is the rivers that divide the region into the various areas which have become household names by virtue of their long history and continued excellence. It is also a region with strong ties to Britain, dating back to the marriage of Eleanor of Aquitaine and Henry Plantagenet.

Climate and geography

Bordeaux enjoys a moderate, humid climate heavily influenced by the proximity of the Atlantic Ocean and the Gironde river.

The traditional Bordeaux blend is of Cabernet Sauvignon and Merlot as a primary varietal, blended with a minority mixture of Cabernet Franc, Petit Verdot, Carmenère and Malbec. These are the six permitted grape types in the region and not all Châteaux make wide use of the minor varietals.

Centuries of wine production have also complicated the rules which govern the labelling of Bordeaux wine. Essentially Bordeaux appellations operate on a scale of increasing specificity with the most broad being AC Bordeaux narrowing to five *Premier*

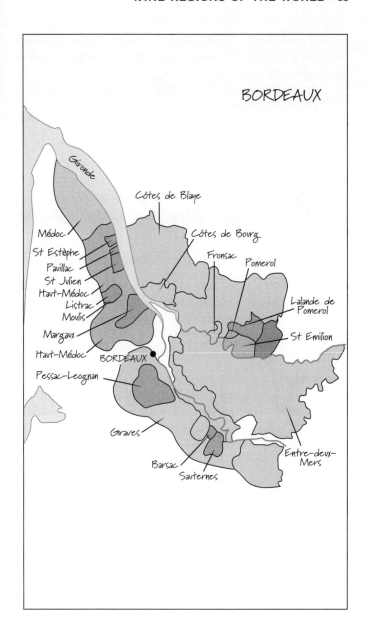

BORDEAUX

Gironde

Côtes de Blaye

Côtes de Bourg

Médoc

St Estèphe

Pauillac

St Julien

Haut-Médoc

Listrac

Moulis

Margaux

Haut-Médoc

Fronsac

Pomerol

Lalande de Pomerol

St Emilion

BORDEAUX

Pessac-Leognan

Graves

Barsac

Sauternes

Entre-deux-Mers

Cru or First Growths. The classifications for these were almost all set down in Paris in 1855, with remarkably few changes to the list of classifications since.

Wine producing areas
Listed below are the wine producing regions of Bordeaux, divided by appellation.

Médoc and Haut-Médoc
The Médoc is divided into two distinct regions north and south of the village of St Estèphe – below lies the Médoc and above the Haut-Médoc. The Haut-Médoc is home to all but one of the wines classified in 1855.

The best communes in the Haut-Médoc (listed from north to south):

- **St Estèphe**
  Reds generally demonstrate a richness of character often attributed to the clay content of the soil. The two greatest AC within this commune are *AC Montrose* and *AC Cos d'Estournel*. *Calon Ségur* has also been a long-time respected Château.

- **Pauillac**
  Three of the most highly esteemed wine houses grew from this unassuming area; *Château Lafite, Latour* and *Mouton Rothschild*. With a remarkable blend of soft-fruit flavours, and heady aromas of wood and tobacco that come from oak aging, they are also set apart by a uniquely dry finish and can occasionally hint at sweetness in the richness of the flavours. Other producers whose wines are well worth trying are *Château Lynch-Bages* and *Château Croizet-Bages*.

- **St Julien**
  Principal wine estates in the area include *Château Gruaud Larose, Château Beychevelle, Château Léoville-Las-Cases* and *Château Léoville Barton*.

Vintage chart: St Julien, Pauillac, St Estèphe

Year	Rating	Year	Rating
2007	86	1993	78
2006	87	1992	79
2005	95	1991	75
2004	88	1990	97
2003	95	1989	90
2002	88	1988	88
2001	88	1987	82
2000	98	1986	94
1999	87	1985	92
1998	87	1983	86
1997	84	1982	98
1996	96	1981	85
1995	92	1980	78
1994	85	1979	85

- **Margaux**

  Grown on a special type of white gravel swept down from the mountains, Margaux is home to a large number of classified growths. Margaux are perhaps best identified by their light, yet gravelly nose which rounds off with a particularly distinctive bouquet. Margaux are often described as very feminine.

Vintage chart: Margaux

Year	Rating	Year	Rating
2007	86	1993	77
2006	88	1992	76
2005	98	1991	74
2004	87	1990	90
2003	88	1989	87
2002	88	1988	85
2001	89	1987	76
2000	95	1986	90
1999	89	1985	86
1998	86	1983	95
1997	82	1982	86
1996	88	1981	82
1995	88	1980	79
1994	85	1979	87

- **Moulis**
  Dominated as the name suggests by Windmills, Moulis tends towards a rather softer, rounder red and is usually the youngest drinking Bordeaux.

- **Listrac**
  A less-fashionable area in the Médoc which produces tannic and powerful red wines perhaps most akin to St Estèphe.

Within these six communes of the Haut-Médoc the top category – *Premier Cru Classé* (First Growths) – covers Five Châteaux:

- **Château Lafite** (From the village of Pauillac)

- **Château Latour** (Also from Pauillac and equally majestic)

- **Château Mouton-Rothschild** (Which became a *Premier Cru* in 1973)

- **Château Margaux**

- **Château Haut-Brion** (This is actually Péssac-Léognan and not Haut-Médoc)

The classification of growths cover first to fifth Cru followed by *Cru Bourgeois* and *Petits Châteaux*, with *Premiers Cru* the most prestigious (and pricey). Within the communes of Bordeaux there are various producers at all these levels of classification, although only ever these five producing First Growths.

Pocket fact 🍷

Through marriage Château Calon-Ségur came to be owned by the Marquis Ségur, the long-time owner of both First Growths Lafite and Latour. However, he claimed that his heart remained in Calon-Ségur and today the label sports a heart around the appellation to signify this.

Graves

Graves is French for gravel, and this is indicative of the soil in this area where both reds and whites are grown to some acclaim. Lying just south of the city of Bordeaux, Cabernet Sauvignon and Merlot dominate the reds whilst Sémillon, Sauvignon Blanc and Muscadelle make up the whites. The best of the vineyards close to Bordeaux bear the appellation AC Pessac-Leognan. The most illustrious of these, *Château Pape Clément* and *Château Haut-Brion*, have been producing fine red and white wines since the Middle Ages, and can claim full credit for placing Bordeaux as one of the leading wine producers of the world.

Pocket fact 🍷

Renowned diarist Samuel Pepys commented in 1663 that he had sampled in London a 'French wine called Ho Bryen that hath a good and most particular taste I never met with'.

For beautiful white wines, try *Château Carbonnieux* which convey aromas of honey, peaches and vanilla within a creamy but firm structure.

Vintage chart: Graves

Year	Rating	Year	Rating
2007	83	1993	86
2006	88	1992	76
2005	94	1991	74
2004	88	1990	90
2003	88	1989	89
2002	87	1988	89
2001	88	1987	84
2000	98	1986	89
1999	87	1985	90
1998	94	1983	89
1997	86	1982	88
1996	86	1981	85
1995	89	1980	78
1994	88	1979	88

Sauternes and Barsac

Wine from the Sauternes is unique in the region of Bordeaux, producing sweet wines from grapes affected by *Botrytis cinerea* (Noble Rot). Clay and limestone soils ensure the dampness which encourages Noble Rot.

Muscadelle, Sémillon and Sauvignon Blanc can be found to varying degrees in Sauternes, creating intensely sweet wines with a beautiful floral fragrance and a deep, golden colour.

Within the area, *Château d'Yquem* is the most revered producer of the finest Sauternes, having been classified in 1855. *Château Lafaurie-Peyraguey* also creates wines that are notable for their floral aromas and sumptuous flavours.

Pocket fact ♀

The most expensive wine ever sold at auction was a 1787 Château Lafite formerly owned by Thomas Jefferson. It was bought for £105,000 in December 1985 at Christie's in London and remains the most expensive wine ever sold.

Pomerol

If you are new to red wines, or to the dark complexity of the Bordeaux produce, then trying a red from the Pomerol area would be a good first step in developing an appreciation of these wines. This is a tiny area alongside AC St Emilion with mainly gravelly soil which produces largely Merlot.

Pomerol reds exhibit the deep colour associated with a full-bodied Bordeaux, but contain less of the acidity and tannin quantity that can make these wines a little heavy for the novice drinker. Instead, Pomerol Bordeaux is gentler on the senses, with plummy flavours and a creamy texture.

To make sure you taste the best this area has to offer, look for the long established estates of *L'Evangile*, *La Conseillante* and *Château La Fleur-Pétrus*, or newcomers *Clos l'Eglise* and *Château Cliret*.

Vintage chart: Pomerol

Year	Rating	Year	Rating
2007	84	1993	87
2006	96	1992	82
2005	95	1991	58
2004	88	1990	95
2003	84	1989	93
2002	85	1988	89
2001	90	1987	85
2000	96	1986	87
1999	87	1985	88
1998	96	1983	90
1997	87	1982	96
1996	85	1981	86
1995	92	1980	79
1994	89	1979	86

St Emilion

A region of winemakers who create fine red wines that are rich, dense and overflowing with ripe fruit flavours from Merlot (60%) and Cabernet Franc (40%).

The classifications of wines from this area have been updated every 10 years since the classification of top châteaux in 1955. Excellent producers may be promoted to *Grand Cru* or even *Premier Grand Cru* status, whilst those whose standards have slipped will be demoted. Top producers of red wine in St Emilion include *Château Cheval Blanc, Clos Saint Martin* and *Château Ausone*.

Vintage chart: St Emilion

Year	Rating	Year	Rating
2007	85	1993	84
2006	90	1992	76
2005	96	1991	59
2004	88	1990	98
2003	90	1989	89
2002	87	1988	88
2001	90	1987	74
2000	98	1986	89
1999	87	1985	88
1998	95	1983	89
1997	86	1982	93
1996	87	1981	82
1995	88	1980	72
1994	86	1979	84

Fronsac, Bourg and Blaye

Less fashionable but good value reds in the Bordeaux style come from Fronsac, with *Cotes de Bourg* and *Cotes de Blaye* making some soft, easy-drinking reds.

One to watch: Château d' Angludet 🍇

Although it can be difficult to pick one recommendation from the wealth of delightful wines in Bordeaux, this Château has been somewhat under-rated, especially having undergone recent regeneration which should see it rise further in stature. Good wines that are a good deal more affordable than First Growths.

Loire Valley

The white grape Chenin Blanc originated in the Loire Valley, and is still a fundamental variety in the region. For reds, the predominantly planted grape is the fragrant Cabernet Franc. Roughly speaking, the wines of the Loire can be divided into categories by the four main areas.

Anjou-Saumur

The region is perhaps best known for *Rosé d'Anjou*, the light summery rosé which has surged in popularity in recent years.

Chenin Blanc predominates here, and there are several appellations under which it is released: AC Anjou Blanc (usually medium dry), AC Savennieres (dry) and AC Coteaux du Layon (sweet, made from grapes with Noble Rot). This grape thrives on the local limestone soils and ages well. Locally, Chenin Blanc is known as Pineau de la Loire.

AC Saumur is also famous for traditional method sparkling white wine made from Chenin Blanc.

Touraine

Touraine can be split between the west, adjoining Saumur, and the east. Red wine predominates in the western areas of Chinon and Bourgueil, where wine is made from Cabernet Franc. Bourgeuil is soft and supple, with a nose of violets and deliciously ripe fruit. Chinon is yet more forward in its lighter variants, although also produces some complex wine capable of aging very well.

To the east lies the white wine area of Vouvray. Châteaux are dotted throughout the hillside amidst sprawling villages set against the backdrop of lush greenery and winding rivers that is the Loire Valley.

The Chenin Blanc grown for *Vouvray* can produce a number of styles of wine from dry to sweet, but all are delicately flavoured with honey, orange, quince and apple.

Central vineyards

Specialising in white wines, Sauvignon Blanc is the main grape grown in the vineyards of Pouilly-sur-Loire, Sancerre and its

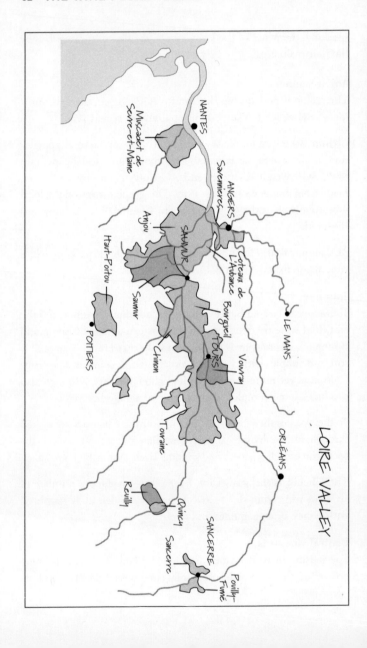

neighbouring villages. The region also dabbles in Pinot Noir from which fairly light reds and successful rosés are produced.

Sancerre is a fine example of the Sauvignon grape's potential to create clean, crisp white wines. *Pouilly-Fumé* benefits from the flinty soil to produce a somewhat lighter bodied wine with greater acidity that can age somewhat better than *Sancerre*. Both have exquisite flavours of lime, apple, peach and apricot, with a chalky minerality.

Haut-Poitou

Haut-Poitou is produced outside of the Loire Valley, near Poitiers, although lacks a distinctive region of its own. Its style is somewhat imitative of *Sancerre* and *Pouilly-Fumé* but substantially cheaper, with whites made from Chardonnay and Sauvignon Blanc. They also produce a soft and supple red from Cabernet Sauvignon and Gamay which is released under the Haut-Poitou appellation.

One to watch: Gaston Huet 🍇

Produces Vouvray with exquisite aromas of melon and honey which meet a dense palate of nutty flavours. Also a producer who makes wine under biodynamic principles (see p. 11).

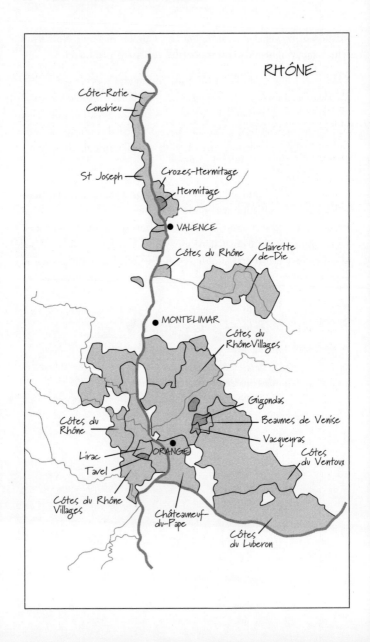

Rhône

This region, producing mainly red wines, is the perfect foil to the predominantly white Loire Valley. Reds from this area are lusciously deep ruby or violet in colour, with concentrated fruit flavours and heavy tannins. Growing is very important in this region, which can still provide excellent value amongst its reds. The finest Rhône wines are suitable for laying down, standing up comparably to the aging potential of the wines of Bordeaux and Burgundy.

Northern Rhône

Although the northern area of the Rhône contains only 10% of the total vineyard area, it produces at least 80% of the best wines. As the steep-sided valley meanders south it channels the Mistral, a strong southerly wind which chills the vines. Syrah is the predominant grape of the Northern Rhône, producing tannic wines with lashings of soft black fruit which age well. Blended wines predominate, with the Rhône producing balanced and lush wines based on Grenache, Syrah and Mourvèdre. Three of the most majestic reds come from:

- **Côte-Rôtie**

    This area literally means 'roasted slope'. Reds have an intense, unctuous flavour of blackberry with aromas of lavender, violet, and the occasional twist of hazelnut. Syrah is the principal grape, blended with up to 20% of the white grape Viognier to produce an elegant red. The best examples come from the vineyards of *Château d'Ampuis*, *Bernard Burgaud* and *Clusel-Roch*.

- **Condrieu**

    Unlike most areas of the Rhône, Condrieu produces both red and white wines of distinction: red wines exhibit strong floral aromas and fresh, pure flavours of dark fruits, and a peppery spice. The whites of AC Condrieu are made solely from Viognier, leaning towards aromas of honeysuckle and baked fruit, with flavours of peach, apricot and almond. For red and white *Domaine de Christian*, *André Perret* and *François Villard* are good producers to look out for.

● **Hermitage**
The red wines of the Hermitage region are heralded in the finest ranks alongside names such as *Château Lafite* and *Romanée-Conti*. Made from 100% Syrah, they have flavours of plums and blackberries, and distinctive elements of spice, but there is subtle differentiation in flavour and style depending on the area in which the grapes are grown. The lightest, most aromatic and potentially most accessible examples of *Hermitage* come from vineyards that lie high on the hill, such as *Beaume* and *L'Hermite*. The lower lying vineyards of *Le Méal* and *Chapoutier* produce more intense, fleshy wines.

Another appellation is that of *Crozes-Hermitage*, with a much wider catchment area than its neighbour. These wines tend to be lighter and more accessible, if a little simpler, with excellent examples from wineries such as *Domaine Marc Sorrel*, *des Remiziéres* and *Domaine Yann Chave*.

● **St Joseph**
These reds are supple with concentrated fruit, although vary along appellation area. Despite using Syrah, they tend towards a lighter style than *Hermitage*. *Jaboullet* and *Gaillard* are extremely consistent producers and *Monteillet* was praised highly by famed critic Robert Parker for its 2004 vintage.

Southern Rhône
● **Châteauneuf-du-Pape** is the centrepiece of the region and producer of highly alcoholic, rich, dense red wines that are high in flavour and quality. Wine produced under this appellation almost exceeds the production of the Northern Rhône, yet maintains an impeccably high standard. Their unique *terroir* ensures ripeness and low acidity in traditional Grenache, Syrah and Mourvèdre blends. Excellent producers include *Beaucastel*

and *Domaines Perrin*. *Clos des Papes* from Paul Avril is also an out-standing if exclusive producer.

Pocket fact 🍷
Châteauneuf-du-Pape is grown in a surface of pudding stones or galets.

Vintage chart: Châteauneuf du Pape

Year	Rating	Year	Rating
2007	93	1993	85
2006	89	1992	78
2005	95	1991	66
2004	90	1990	94
2003	91	1989	95
2002	65	1988	88
2001	96	1987	61
2000	98	1986	78
1999	91	1985	88
1998	98	1983	87
1997	82	1982	70
1996	82	1981	88
1995	93	1980	77
1994	86	1979	88

● **Lirac and Tavel**
West of Châteauneuf are AC *Lirac* and *Tavel*. Tavel produces what some have called the best rosé in France using Grenache and Cinsault. Top producers include *Domaine Lafond-Roc-Epine*. AC Lirac produces some similar rosé but also a rich, supple and spicy red made from predominantly Syrah and Mourvèdre. Top producers include *Chateau d'Aqueria* with some real value to be found in this appellation.

● **Gigondas**
Lying at the bottom of the Dentelles de Monmirail mountains, Gigondas is home to some balanced yet robust red wines

which are an excellent value counter-part to *Châteauneuf-du-Pape*. The area's best output is earthy and spicy, using principally Grenache but also Syrah and Mourvèdre to create rustic but charming wines.

- **Vacqueyras**
  Dark and rich whilst displaying herbal and spice notes, *Vacqueyras* is one of the finest villages of the Rhone. Look out for characteristic full and smooth wines at reasonable prices.

The Southern Rhône is also the centre for AC Côtes-du-Rhône production, a generic appellation which houses a broad variety of reds. Try Côtes-du-Rhône villages for a more reliably enjoyable wine. These reds can represent excellent value, often filling out the lower end of wine lists and worth exploring. Look out for excellent wines from *Chapoutier* and *Les Jamelles*.

Pocket fact 🍷

Rhône bottles are a unique shape and almost always have an 'embossed' logo.

One to watch:
Domaine du Vieux Télégraphe 🍇

Creates some of the finest Châteauneuf-du-Pape on the market from one single block of vineyards. Their luscious reds display aromatic herbal noses alongside ripe fruit, which meet a silken body with lashings of deep, dense fruit and ripe tannins.

Alsace

As the border province of France and Germany, this region is very much split between the two. The combination of Germanic climate and soil, coupled with a distinctively French approach to winemaking results in some truly fabulous white wines.

The cooler climate of Alsace separates it from the other wine regions of France in that it encourages growth of both traditional German and French varieties. The best vineyards in Alsace grow only:

Riesling	Makes the best wines in all of the Alsace region, traditionally dry.
Gewürztraminer	This grape yields delicate wines that are a perfect introduction to the style of Alsace.
Muscat	Wines from this grape are here made into wonderfully dry wines that make an excellent aperitif.
Pinot Gris	Creates full-bodied wines that are a good alternative to white Burgundy.

Vendanges Tardive (late harvest) have a higher alcoholic content and are dry to medium sweet, whilst *Séléctions de grains nobles* (Noble Rot grapes) denotes a sweet wine, often made from *Grand Cru* grapes.

Top producers include *Kuentz-Bas*, *Hugel* and the ubiquitous co-operative *Turckheim*.

One to watch: Zind Humbrecht 🍇

Lind Humbreacht's Pinot Gris and Gewürztraminer are joyful. The former shows quite soft acidity and perfumed fruit on the palate, with lush tropical fruit. The latter exudes lychee fruit, with a beautiful creamy palate which is balanced with good acidity and lush yet clean fruit.

Languedoc-Roussillon

Nestled in the south of the country, the Languedoc Roussillon is the most concentrated vineyard area in the world. With a long history of wine-growing and proud defence of a regional agricultural lifestyle, the winegrowers of the south have earned a fiery reputation to match their often powerful reds. There is scope for finding real value amongst the produce of the south however, as it is often overlooked in favour of more prestigious areas.

Fitou/Corbieres/Minervois

These neighbouring appellations produce a range of good to excellent wines in the areas once notorious for over-production and cultivation since Caesar first took Gaul. They are dominated by the cooperative *Mont Tauch,* which produces some excellent high-end wines alongside decent-value reds. Carignan and Grenache dominate the blends and despite regional variation one can depend on a meaty red dominated by blueberry notes with herbal undertones. *Minervois* is leading the way in terms of utilising better varieties in blends and drinks like a refined *Corbieres*. Excellent value can be had with *Château Maris, Château de Cesseras* and *Comte Câthare* – all from the north of the Minervois.

Costières de Nîmes/Coteaux de Languedoc

Campuget is an excellent mass-market Nîmes producer, whilst there are a wealth of good independents to explore across these areas of powerful yet nuanced reds. *Château de la Negly*, for example, is producing a beautifully inky-black blend accentuated by spices and pepperiness. Coteaux de Languedoc is also producing some crisp whites from *Picpould de Pinet*, a variety which has come of age in recent years. Try *Domaines Félines Jourdan* for an excellent example.

Pocket fact ♉

Bottles of Costières de Nîmes generally bear an alligator bound to a palm tree, signifying the conquest of Egypt by Rome and harking back to coins minted by the Romans for use in the South of France.

Pic St Loup

Originally just a commune of the Coteaux de Languedoc, this area has earned its own reputation for excellence. With blends coming from roughly 90% noble varieties (Grenache, Syrah and Mourvèdre) and at least six-year-old vines, this promises the best the Midi has to offer. Producers such as *Domaine de l'Hortus* are leading the charge for international recognition.

Faugeres/St-Chinian

Just north of Béziers lie the more local ACs of *Faugères* and *St-Chinian*, two of the hidden gems of the South. Syrah, Grenache and Mourvèdre plantations create beautifully expressive wines dominated by blackberry fruit, liquorice and cigar box aromas which develop. Excellent examples include *Domaines Leon Barral* in Faugeres and *Domaine Belles Courbes* in St-Chinian.

Blanquette de Limoux

The first recorded sparkling white and quite possibly the model for Champagne, with Dom Pérignon apparently passing through the Limoux on his way from Spain. Made entirely from Mauzac and Chardonnay this sparkling is a joyfully creamy textured white with balanced acidity. Some prefer this to its Northern neighbour and it certainly streaks ahead in terms of value. The Crémant version also includes Chenin Blanc, for a boosted note of lush honeyed fruit.

Côtes du Roussillon-Villages

A vast area of basic gutsy red production, the addition of the suffix *Villages* denotes a smaller area and better quality. Further to this, *Les Aspres* indicates one of the 23 communes which have committed to using improved varietals, with a maximum of 25% Carignan. Excellent producers include *Domaine Gauby* and *Domaine Boucabeille*.

Muscat de Rivesaltes
Dating back to the 13th century, this was possibly the first *vin doux naturel* produced in France. A sweet, fortified white wine made from a blend of *Muscat a petits grains* and *Muscat d'Alexandrie* and drunk widely as an aperitif. Bottled young to preserve the fresh fruit characters amongst the sweetness, it should be drunk in kind.

Other south-western
Some 160km south of Bordeaux, yet further west than the Rhône, *AC Madiran* is something of a peculiarity. The principal grape is Tannat – a difficult grape with high tannins and astringent notes – which is often blended with Cabernet Sauvignon and Cabernet Franc to produce a more welcoming wine. Some of these wines age very well, and display notes of rich black fruits, tobacco, spices and smoky roasted coffee when ready after five or six years. The delightfully named AC Buzet is another area to watch for value, with very decent Bordeaux-blend reds, aromatic whites and rich, fruity rosés necessitating a mention.

One to watch:
Domaine Belles Courbes 🍇

This passionate producer is not averse to innovation. He produces an outstanding St Chinan, which shows impressive body balanced with supple fruits and an aromatic character borne out by vanilla oak. Domaine Belles Courbes is also responsible for an excellent oak-aged rosé with a spicy nose and round, supple palate that yields ripe red fruit and a hint of oaky vanilla.

⤜ GERMANY ⤛

HISTORY

German whites were once the toast of London, but were then derided. Nevertheless, devotees maintain that Germany produces excellent value wines which can only improve in their popularity. A long and illustrious wine history stretching back to Roman times ensures that production maintains high standards despite the challenges of the climate. Producers are starting to win back consumers with a taste for something different by modernising their appeal, and their labels.

CLIMATE AND GEOGRAPHY

The majority of Germany's grapevines lie as far north as grapes can feasibly grow, along the banks of the river Rhine and its tributaries. Although this terrain seems inhospitable at best for the vine, it produces grapes that have such a rare balance of sugar and acidity as to produce soft poetic wines.

GRAPE VARIETIES

White

- **Riesling**
  The primary white grape of Germany, which produces delicately aromatic, elegantly fruity wines that vary from very dry to very sweet.

- **Müller-Thurgau, Silvaner.**

Red

- **Spätburgunder** (Pinot Noir)
  Produces round, fruity wines from late-harvesting grapes that perform best in Pfalz and Baden.

KEY WINE PRODUCING AREAS

Germany has 13 distinct wine producing regions, each of which is then broken down into more specific regions. The most important of these are listed below.

Mosel-Saar-Ruwer

The confluence of the Mosel, Saar and Ruwer rivers creates one of Germany's most important wine regions where distinctive tall green bottles are filled with delightful Riesling. Although cool temperatures leave quality highly dependent upon vintage, warmer years can produce perfumed and delicate whites and this has been the trend over the past decade.

Pocket fact 🍷

Many vineyards in this region belong to religious and charitable bodies due to ancient land-rights. Look out particularly for wines from Friedrich-Wilhelm-Gymnasium as this was Karl Marx's old school!

Rheingau

Home of magnificent vineyards that flank the Rhine. There are three notable areas within this region:

● **Assmannshausen**
  Growers have cultivated Spätburgunder with very promising results, producing deep, full-bodied reds with a smoky aroma.

● **Central Rheingau**
  The traditional wines from the Rheingau region are the remarkable and super-sweet *Beerenauslesen* and *Trockenbeerenauslesen* styles of Riesling. These wines, so well reputed in both the

domestic and international market, still command the highest prices, but since the 1990s producers have increasingly embraced the trend for dry wines.

● **Hochheim**

The vineyards lie on the far east of the region, in a fairly isolated position. This is the main region for producing *Hock*. The warmth imbues the wines with a greater body and earthiness, along with more distinctive fruit flavours than is usually found in German wines. Good producers from this region include *Kirchenstück*, *Franz Künstler* and *Reiner Flick*.

Pocket fact 🍷

Wines from Hocheim were nicknamed Hock by Queen Victoria, whose penchant for the rounded whites didn't extend as far as learning how to pronounce them.

Rheinhessen

One of the few areas in Germany where Riesling doesn't predominate, allowing space for Müller-Thurgau and Silvaner to shine. Avoid the sickly and ubiquitous *Liebfraumilch* and instead try some of the produce of the central Rheinterrasse near the towns of Oppenheim and Nierstein, where red sandstone soil makes for some excellent Riesling. Top producers include *Heyl zu Hernsheim* and *Gunderloch*.

Pfalz

Close to the French border, this area is the most productive wine region in Germany and also the home to Germany's finest reds, where alluvial soil offers plumpness to the fruit. Riesling production is also widespread and of varying quality. Look out for Weinstraβe (Wine Route) appended to the label, as this is home to some excellent small vineyards.

Baden

Between Freiburg and the Rhine, volcanic soil aids excellent cultivation of Müller-Thurgau and Spätburgunder. Also worth exploration is a pale rosé wine from the region known as Weißherbst, made from black grapes with great finesse.

> *One to watch: Hermann Dönnhoff* 🍇
>
> *This excellent winemaker produces some fantastic Riesling, in particular the Spätlese is worth trying – good acidity with pronounced mineral notes and lush citrus fruit flavours alongside a delightful white floral nose.*

⊶ GREECE ⊷

Historically important if a little less popular today, Greece produces a wealth of wines. The Peloponnese produce many famous dessert wines including *Muscat of Patras* and the red *Mavrodaphne of Patras*. There are also two dry whites of note: *Mantineia*, which produces subtle, aromatic whites with a hint of rose petal, and *Patras*, which also produces youthful, aromatic whites from the Roditis grape.

In Macedonia, the *Naousa* cultivation of the Xynomavro grape makes excellent full-bodied tannic reds with plenty of spice and a distinct savoury note. Its neighbour, *Goumenissa,* also produces excellent reds from this grape.

Attica, in central Greece, is the biggest producing region. Mostly white wine is produced from local grape varieties, yet by far the most famous is *Retsina*, which is flavoured with pine resin – most definitely an acquired taste. In the islands, Crete produces much table wine for the home market whilst *Santorini* is famous for its whites and *Samos* produces a white dessert Muscat famous in France.

One to watch: Domaine Tselepos 🍇

This small winery produces some excellent examples of indigenous Greek grapes. Try Moschofilero from its Maninian estate — soft rose petals on the nose are accompanied by a refreshing grapefruit and citrus palate that is both fresh and delightful.

⟶┤ ISRAEL ├⟵

Much Israeli viticulture restarted after the Baron de Rothschild gave a foundation grant to the country's winegrowers. The five regions of Israeli winemaking are: *Galilee*, containing the Golan Heights where altitude lends much needed acidity to the wines; *Samaria*, where significant investment has been made near Mount Carmel to increase quality and encourage wine-tourism; *Samson*, where Cabernet Sauvignon and Merlot single varietals have attracted international praise; the *Judean Hills*, including hillside trained vineyards which produce good wines; and *Negev*, where near-desert conditions necessitate drip irrigation. A large proportion of Israeli wine production is turned over to the production of kosher wine.

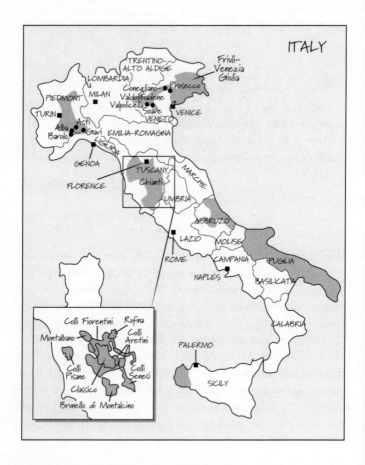

~| ITALY |~

HISTORY

If the Romans were the founding fathers of winemaking as we know it today, it comes as no surprise that the Italians have a gift when it comes to producing the ruby nectar (and its golden counterpart).

Italy has the most extensive variety of individual wine styles, differing local climates and indigenous grapes of all the winemaking countries in the world. Because of this, the quality of wine can prove as temperamental as the flavours created across the country. Italian wines range from inimitably stylish, stimulating wines to those produced with a distinctive lack of creative flair.

CLIMATE AND GEOGRAPHY

The country has a backbone of mountains running right down from north to south, creating plots at every desirable altitude and exposure level for most grape varieties. Moreover, the landscape consists of volcanic soil that ensures fantastic natural drainage for vines. The terrain throughout Italy is conducive and varied, just like the wines themselves.

GRAPE VARIETIES

White

Moscato, Trebbiano, Soave, Cortese, Chardonnay, Pinot Grigio, Garganega.

Red

Sangiovese, Nebbiolo, Bonarda, Barbera, Dolcetto, Brunello, Corvina.

KEY WINE PRODUCING AREAS

The winemaking regions of Italy are numerous and varied, and to explore them all would be worthy of a book to themselves. The main ones are listed below.

Tuscany

Bordered on the west by the Tyrrhenian Sea and on the east by the Apennines, the geography and climate of Tuscany are so suitable for vine growing that wild varieties have been growing there for centuries.

During the great Italian Renaissance, the Medici family transformed Tuscany into a centre of culture and art. The resulting wines that have been produced since this era are each, in themselves, a work of art.

Chianti

Chianti is traditionally made from the three grape varieties of Sangiovese, Canaiolo and Malvasia Blanca, and must contain at least 70% Sangiovese to be classified as Chianti.

There are seven Chianti subzones: Rufina (the smallest zone), Montalbano, Colli Pisane (by the sea and producing the lightest wines), Colli Senesi (the largest area), Colli Fiorentini, Colli Aretini and Classico (the best-known).

Chianti Classico contains at least 80% Sangiovese, and bottles are marked with the distinctive Black Rooster logo as an indication of authenticity and quality.

Chianti has enjoyed a resurgence in quality of late, with many excellent producers leading the charge for quality. *Isole e Olena* is an excellent Classico vineyard as are *Castello dei Rampolla* and *Fontodi*.

Brunello di Montalcino

Made from Brunello, a clone of Sangiovese, this powerful red demands significant bottle aging. At their best, these wines can compete with Barolo and offer a complex yet delightful bouquet. *Rossi di Montalcino* operates as a second appellation for Brunello producers, allowing them to release younger more saleable wines with brighter fruit characteristics.

Vintage chart: Brunello di Montalcino

Year	Rating	Year	Rating
2007	93	1993	86
2006	94	1992	76
2005	92	1991	85
2004	96	1990	90
2003	90	1989	76
2002	75	1988	89
2001	91	1987	73
2000	94	1986	84
1999	90	1985	93
1998	92	1983	80
1997	95	1982	86
1996	80	1981	82
1995	88	1980	71
1994	86	1979	76

Super Tuscans

The name given to any red wine produced in Tuscany which does not adhere to regional blending rules. Producers such as *Tenuto San Guido* produce excellent wines that flout the appellation laws of the area and innovate. Its *Sassicaia* is a fine Bordeaux blend.

Vin Santo

This dessert wine is made from Trebbiano and Malvasia to produce a beautifully honeyed, sweet nectar, which is made from grapes dried on rush mats before fermentation to concentrate sugar levels.

Vernaccia di San Gimignano

An incredibly historic wine dating back to as early as 1276, this crisp white shows good acidity and citrus fruits.

One to watch: Giuseppe Sesti 🍇

An interesting producer, who tries to reassert the influence of the moon on his organically grown Brunello. The results are impressive and his Altezza release shows ripe red cherries accompanied by deep black fruit and spicy notes on the nose with an earthy, plummy palate.

Piedmont

Lying at the confluence of the Tanaro and Barbera rivers, and sandwiched between the Alps to the north and the Apennines to the south, Piedmont has a varied year-round climate that is far from Mediterranean but does benefit from hot summers for grape ripening.

- **Alba**

  Home to some very grand Italian red wines, all of which are made with varying quantities of the Nebbiolo grape.

•	Barolo	Named after the village in which it is made, this wine consists predominantly of the Nebbiolo grape, and barrel aged for a minimum of two years. Creates deep, intelligent wines with blackcurrant aromas that are known in Italy as 'The King of Wines'. Producers are split between Modernists and Traditionalists, with the former producing slicker and more rounded wines and the latter upholding a fuller-bodied more muscular style. Excellent Modernist producers include Giorgio Rivetti and Chiari Boschis. For a taste of tradition seek out Bruno Giacosa and Marcarini.
•	Barbaresco	Made with 100% Nebbiolo this is a full, fragrant, mellow wine with rich blackcurrant aromas. Benefits from aging, and those from *Roero Arnis* are considered amongst the finest. Barolo's sister wine.
•	Gattinara	Also mainly Nebbiolo, but with up to 10% Bonarda in the blend. Similar wines to Barolo operating at a lower end of the market.
•	Barbera	Produces a young, fresh and fruity red that shows good acidity.
•	Dolcetto	The name means 'little sweet one', and it is often soft and fruity although some producers have begun to make more full-bodied offerings.

Vintage chart: Barolo

Year	Rating	Year	Rating
2007	91	1993	86
2006	89	1992	72
2005	92	1991	76
2004	96	1990	96
2003	92	1989	96
2002	75	1988	90
2001	88	1987	85
2000	88	1986	78
1999	94	1985	90
1998	86	1983	75
1997	94	1982	92
1996	95	1981	80
1995	87	1980	71
1994	77	1979	86

- **Asti**
  Encircled by hills that give protection from sunlight and create a cooler climate, this area provides the white counterpart to the might of the Alba reds. It is particularly famed for its sweet, floral, sparkling whites made from the Moscato grape. *Moscato d'Asti* epitomises the saccharine quality of this region's most predominant exports.

- **Gavi**
  Made from the Cortese grape in the Southern hillside around the town of Gavi, this wine has become a popular export from this region. With a steely lime zing, it is a fresh yet complex dry white of which there are excellent examples widely available.

One to watch: Fontanafreddo 🍇
A well-established estate in the Piedmont region, which produces good-quality examples of Barolo, Barbara, Dolcetto and Barbaresca wines.

Veneto

The rolling hills around the city of Verona are not only the setting for Shakespeare's most famous love story, but also that of some fabulous Italian vineyards. The fertile volcanic soil of the region encourages vines to run riot over the landscape, allowing Veneto to take the title of Italy's most productive wine region.

- **Soave**

  Made from the Garganega grape, which exhibits delicacy in both its fruit and acidity with a touch of almond. However, the extent of Trebbiano in the blend can often render the wine uninteresting and neutral at lower prices. Treat yourself to a *Soave Classico* or *Recioto di Soave Superiore* to experience its true persona. *Pieropan* is probably the best producer around.

- **Valpolicella**

  Blended from the black grape Corvina (which imparts the sour cherry flavour) with Rondinella and Molinara to produce a smooth, fruity red with a savoury bite. *Ripasso*-style Valpollicella is quite different from the *Normale*, with the grape juice passed over dried skins during fermentation to add extra body and concentration of fruit flavours.

  Amarone della Valpolicella is far more distinguished and is made using semi-dried grapes to produce a characteristically intense and long raisiny finish. *Quintarelli* and *Speri* make excellent examples. These can be difficult to pair with food and are often recommended by locals for drinking alone.

- **Prosecco**

  A sparkling white wine made from a grape of the same name, Prosecco is increasingly gaining a reputation as a palatable and inexpensive alternative to Champagne. The price difference is due to a second fermentation in tanks (known as the Charmat method) as opposed to the bottle fermentation which produces the fizz in *Méthode Champenoise*.

Prosecco displays fresh and apparent fruit with the emphasis on youthful drinking. In the model of Champagne, Prosecco is served *Brut* (Extra-dry), Extra-Dry (quite-dry) and Dry (confusingly off-dry).

The best Prosecco comes from the hillside district of Conegliano-Valdobbiadene and is left on the lees to develop a creamy mouth feeling. The *Grand Cru* of the region is Cartizze, which tends towards sweeter wines due to its hilltop position and resultant ripeness of fruit. Top producers include the giant *Bisol* and also *La Farra*.

One to watch: Quintarelli 🍇

Often known as the 'Master of the Veneto', this producer excels in releasing some of the very best Amarone on the market. There are excellent value entry-level blends such as Primo Fiore as well as outstanding releases such as Alzero and Rosso del Bepi.

Friuli-Venezia Giulia

The most revered areas in this hillside region bordering the Balkans are *Colli Orientali del Friuli* and *Collio Goriziano*, both noted for fresh, dry white wines made from the Tocai Friulana grape, as well as blends from the more common Sauvignon Blanc, Pinot Grigio and Pinot Bianco varieties. Although this area is responsible for only 2% of Italian produce, it is an important quality wine area, with 50% of the region's output of DOCG status. Moderated by cool winds blowing from the Alps, this region is ideally placed to produce crisp, fruity wines displaying excellent varietal characteristics.

Verduzzo is grown to produce honeyed fragrant wines which retain dryness alongside their perfume. It is also used to produce *Ramondolo,* a full-bodied dessert wine.

The *Isonzo* region lies to the south of Collio along the Isonzo river and is subject to greater rainfall than its northern counterpart. This leads to a greater speciality in producing sparkling wines, of particular note is the Pinot Bianco. Chardonnay and Malvasia are also grown in a dry style in this region. Likewise, the southern *Friuli-Grave* produces many attractive dry whites along similar lines and using Sauvignon Blanc.

There are also some quality reds from the Friuli-Venezia Giulia region. Using principally Refosco, Merlot and Schioppettino, producers such as *Ronco del Gnemiz* and *Ronchi di Cialla* have produced deep, dark spicy reds with ripe black fruit flavours and perfumed noses.

One to watch: Jermann 🍇

Produces high-end Pinot Grigio that demonstrates the potential of the region by exhibiting the aromatic character of the grape to the full. Long and complex, Jermann's aged releases are characterised by lingering orange zest and dry walnut flavours on the palate.

Abbruzo

Rich, fruity and low in tannin, the wines of Montepulciano d'Abbruzzo are popular and common in Britain. They are usually a reliable choice for restaurant drinking, often hovering around the lower end of the wine list, and producers such as *Valentini* excel.

Puglia

Salice Salentino is a DOC increasingly seen in export markets, as it has made a name for itself amongst the overproduction of Italy's heel. This is a deep red which combines Negroamaro and Malvasian Nero to produce tart cherry notes alongside a restrained body. This is an excellent food wine and usually reasonably priced.

Sicily

This is the largest area under vine in Italy's provinces, producing much simple table wine but also some quality reds from the interior mountainous region around Etna. *Planeta* are probably the best producer but the *Settesoli* cooperative is also worth trying. Zinfandel, Nero D'Avola, Merlot, Syrah and Cabernet Sauvignon dominate the reds, whilst there are good whites made from Chardonnay, Viognier and Grillo. Sicily is also the home to *Marsala*, the sweet fortified wine which can show elegant complexity.

One to watch: Marco de Bartoli 🍇

A revered Sicilian producer who harnessed the best of the Sicilian viticultural possibilities in the flavours of his wines. For an authentic experience, try the Marco de Bartoli Bukkuram Sicily Moscato.

~~| LEBANON |~~

A long and proud tradition accompanies much quality production today. The Bekaa Valley is by far the most important region, where the iconic *Château Musar* produces excellent Bordeaux blends. Bordeaux and Rhone varietals somewhat dominate in terms of planting, with Cabernet Sauvignon, Cabernet Franc, Merlot, Grenache, Cinsault and Carignan prevailing.

Much of Lebanese winemaking bears the hallmark of French influence, although there is also some cultivation of local blends, which usually perform well.

~~| NEW ZEALAND |~~

HISTORY

Winemaking was introduced to New Zealand by the British colonisers in the 19th century, but due to the focus on farming meat for export and the British preference for beer over wine, it was only made in very small quantities for domestic use.

It was only very recently that global economic developments encouraged New Zealand to start forging out its own niche in the world wine market. In 1973, when Britain entered the European Economic Community, they were forced to relinquish their hold over the New Zealand export business. This subsequently allowed New Zealand to begin to explore more lucrative export possibilities outside of the traditional meat industry. This was when they started to make wine in earnest.

Pocket fact 🍷

In 1960 New Zealand was home to only 1,000 acres of vineyards, whereas nowadays this has expanded to over 54,000 acres and 560 producers.

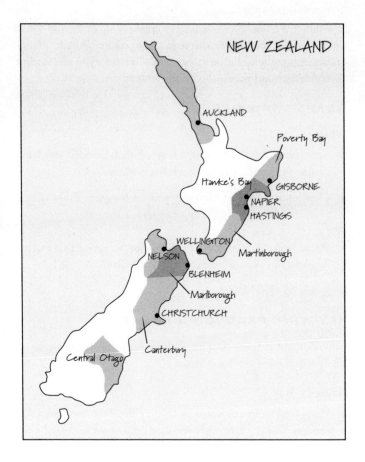

CLIMATE AND GEOGRAPHY

Cooled by prevailing westerly winds from the Pacific Ocean and naturally irrigated by the rain-clouds which gather over the extensive mountain ranges, New Zealand has a climate that is considerably chillier than that usually associated with fine wine-growing territories.

It is this that allows New Zealand to create some of the most distinctive wines on the world stage. The cooler climate allows grapes, especially white varieties, to take on a zesty, acidic quality that adds bite and personality to the wines.

GRAPE VARIETIES

White

- Sauvignon Blanc: This was the grape that founded the New Zealand reputation for uniquely lively wines.

- Chardonnay, Riesling, Gewürztraminer, Viognier, Pinot Gris.

Red

- Pinot Noir: A notoriously tricky grape to grow, this variety flourishes in the cool climate of New Zealand.

- Syrah, Merlot, Malbec.

KEY WINE PRODUCING AREAS

New Zealand is home to nine distinct wine producing regions. The most notable are listed below.

Hawke's Bay

- Vines have been cultivated in this region since the mid 19th century, making it one of New Zealand's most historical viticultural areas.

- It was in the 1990s that Hawke's Bay wines were put on the international map. A combination of very dry, hot summers and an increased understanding of the most suitable soils from which to grow healthy vines, resulted in some incredibly full red wines with substantial tannin levels that could stand up to aging without losing their characteristic New Zealand twang.

- Malbec and Syrah thrive in this region, and a good example of the flavours can be found in the succulently fruity Syrah from *Brookfields Hillside*.

Martinborough

- A report in 1979 likened the soil and climate of Martinborough to Burgundy. Since that moment Burgundian style output and Pinot Noir have dominated.

- This region enjoys a cool climate throughout the year, but has some of the greatest temperature fluctuations from day to night in the country, and also enjoys particularly dry autumns. These factors combine to create a superb environment in which the Pinot grape can flourish.

- Pinot Noirs from this region can range from incredibly rich and plummy through to exhibiting more complex dry, earthy qualities.

- Pinot Gris is also beginning to emerge as producing strong wines in this area and is worth keeping an eye on.

- Leading wineries include *Ata Rangi, Dry River* and *Martinborough Vineyard*.

Marlborough

- This small region that sits atop the northernmost point of the South Island is home to almost half of New Zealand's vineyards.

- The Sauvignon Blanc produced here has become world famous. They have markedly defined, easy to understand flavours that are both a pleasure for the connoisseur and a god-send for the beginner, as they provide a great baseline from which to start learning how to define flavours.

- Chardonnay and Pinot Noir are also grown extensively, and are used in the delightful sparkling wines that come from this region.

Central Otago

- As the world's southernmost wine region, Central Otago boasts a continental climate that is almost unique compared to any other area of New Zealand.

- Summers are sunny, although short, and sitting as it does directly below the hole in the ozone layer allows powerful bursts of sunshine on the grapes. Couple this with cool night temperatures and again a climate that seems to foster Pinot Noir is created.

- Pinot Noir from this region tends to have bright fruit flavours and is created from extremely ripe grapes creating powerful and rather alcoholic wines.

One to watch: Kim Crawford Wines

A stand-out amongst the flood of Kiwi Sauvignon Blancs. Its stunning Sauvignon has a delightful grapefruit note on the nose and a zingy citrus palate underwritten by balanced mineral notes.

⊶ PORTUGAL ⊷

HISTORY

Despite being perched on the periphery of Europe, Portugal proved itself an individualistic country when it came to wine production, and instead of embracing the grapes of France as most of Europe proved disposed to do, it stuck to producing wine with its own inimitable indigenous varieties. Initially, wine production with these unique grapes was limited to the production of port. Nowadays many varieties are now being used to create voluptuous red wines and aromatic whites.

CLIMATE AND GEOGRAPHY

Portugal is susceptible to contrary weather conditions created by both the Atlantic and Mediterranean onto which it faces. Cross-continental weather likewise exercises various unpredictable effects upon the climate. Geology and soil also vary across the country, from seemingly inhospitable granite in the north to soft limestone in the south.

GRAPE VARIETIES

Portugal has numerous grape varieties, the principal of which are listed below.

Red

- Touriga Nacional: this is the signature grape of Portugal that is regarded as the founding grape of port.

- Tinta Periz, Baga, Caselão Frances and Tinto Cão.

White

- Arinto: the white answer to Touriga Nacional, this is a versatile variety that ages well to produce majestic wines.

● Loureiro, Albariño and Bical.

KEY WINE PRODUCING AREAS

Bairrada

● Located in the south west of Portugal, this is one of the country's most well-established wine regions.

● The dominant grape grown is Baga, which creates heavy wines that are high in tannins and acid with a fruity as opposed to vegetal character. They benefit from at least 10 years of bottle aging to mellow fully.

● 85% of the wines produced here are red. The heavy, clay soil lends itself to creating deep reds that express the earthy qualities of their origins. Indeed, the name Bairrada comes from the Portuguese '*bairro*' for clay.

Dão

● Since the 1990s, this region has been developing some of Portugal's most tantalisingly fruity red wines.

● Because the vineyards are set atop a plateau of granite, wines tend to exhibit distinctive stony or mineral flavours and retain high residual sugar levels.

● Most grapes grown in this region are blended in order to create wines with desired characteristics of each, and this has resulted in some lively, fruity reds and beautifully fragrant whites.

● Producers to look out for include *Quinta des Carvalhais*, *Quinta da Pellada* and *Quinta des Roques*.

Estremadura and Setúbal Peninsula

Estremadura is Portugal's most productive wine region, despite not being the largest. It mostly creates easy-drinking, inexpensive wines, although there are some lovely crisp white wines from the Arinto grape which come from this area under the DOCs of Palmela and Arrabida.

Alentejo

Traditionally the preserve of the home market, the fruity, well-balanced whites and reds from the region have started to gain acclaim on the international market. Producers to look out for include *Herdado de Esporão* and *Quinto do Carmo*.

Douro

- As the home of port, this region creates vintages that are of such quality as to be able to stand shoulder to shoulder with the finest wines made around Europe. There are six varieties that you should be aware of:

Vintage	Made from grapes of a select vintage that has been deemed particularly conducive to creating a fine and lasting port. Vintage ports are aged in barrels for a couple of years before being bottled and left to mature for anything up to a further 30 years.
Late Bottled Vintage (LBV)	This had been destined to become vintage port, but lack of demand meant it wasn't bottled and was instead left in the barrel for a further two to four years. Although not of quite the same finesse as a true vintage port, it is not a bad poor man's alternative.
Tawny	Denotes a very pale, very smooth old port that has been aged in wood for anywhere between 10 and 40 years.
Colheita	These are a type of Tawny that are made from a single grape vintage and aged in oak.
Ruby	Ruby ports are aged for a far shorter period than their Tawny counterparts, and as such have less depth of flavour but are still perfectly enjoyable.

- Traditionally, table wines were created as an afterthought in this region, and made from the grapes that were left over from the port harvest. Nowadays, producers are a bit more savvy and have realised that producing a good table wine requires using better quality grapes.

- As a result, the quality of table wines produced in the Douro have markedly improved, and red wines in particular are worth sampling. Look out for the Burgundian-esque reds from producer *Niepoort*, or the complex oak-aged reds from the *Qunita do Vale Donna Maria*.

Pocket fact ♟

One of Portugal's most famous wines, the Vinho Verde, *also has one of the most misleading names. Meaning 'green wine', this beverage is in fact lightly sparkling, and the term 'green' refers only to its youthful and slightly naïve fruit flavours. Almost all exports are white, but there is some red production in this area.*

Madeira

- This volcanic island situated between the Portuguese and African coasts is home to the most unique of the fortified wines.

- Located in the middle of an ancient trade route, the story goes that Madeira wine was discovered when sailors took wine made on the island and fortified it with additional alcohol on board their ships, where it was exposed to extreme heat over the sea voyage. Apparently it was this prolonged baking in the sunshine that allowed Madeira to develop its inimitable flavours.

- There are five kinds of Madeira on the market:

Malmsey	Made primarily from sweet Malvasia grapes, this is the most celebrated form of Madeira, loved for its rich, caramel flavours. It is particularly yummy with a decadent dessert such as chocolate mousse.

Bual	Nutty and sticky, this variety is made predominantly from the Bual grape, which is slightly less sweet than the Malvasia. This makes the best alternative to port, and is good with a cheese course.
Verdelho	Verdelho Madeira, made from the eponymous grape variety, is a medium-dry wine that works best as an unusual accompaniment to seafood.
Sercial	The driest of the five varieties, this should be served chilled and as an aperitif or as an accompaniment to extremely light dishes. A good combination is Sercial with sushi.
Tinta Negra Mole	Unlike the other Madeiras which are all made from a white grape, this is from the red Tinta Negra Mole grape. It varies in style from dry to sweet, and is available at three, five and 10 years old.

One to watch: Quinta do Crasto 🍇

One of Portugal's top winemakers, its Reserva is blended from a wide range of varietals and oak aged to produce a sumptuous, deep red with hints of tobacco and ripe black cherry.

⊶ SOUTH AFRICA ⊷

HISTORY

For most of the 20th century, South African winemaking was stifled under the oppressive constraints of a national cooperative called the KWV that imposed universal prices and controls on wines with no regard for quality.

These sanctions were lifted in the 1970s, heralding a new freedom for South African winemakers who, for the first time, began to travel the world in order to learn new techniques and gain valuable inspiration. Likewise, the end of Apartheid in 1994 increased South Africa's ability to market its wines on the world stage.

Today, South African producers have begun to form their own distinct styles of wine which are beginning to rank favourably at an international level.

CLIMATE AND GEOGRAPHY

A close to Mediterranean temperature is cooled to perfection by the Benguela Current which sweeps up from Antarctica and lowers the temperature over the western coast.

Rainfall is usually limited to the winter months. Generally, the threat of mildew and rot on vines is wiped out by the famous Cape Doctor wind that sweeps through the mountains and blows the fungi away.

Pocket fact 🍷

Baboons are one of the greatest threats to vineyards growing Pinot Noir. Winegrowers have to erect electric fences to keep out the apes that apparently prefer this to any other grape!

GRAPE VARIETIES

Red

Cabernet Sauvignon, Cabernet Franc, Cinsaut, Merlot, Pinotage, Pinot Noir, Shiraz, Zinfandel.

White

Chardonnay, Chenin Blanc (known locally as Steen), Colombard, Sauvignon Blanc.

And there are also a few lesser known varieties.

Cape Riesling

Produces wines with steely, mineral qualities that need a little maturing to develop a more pleasing honey flavour.

Rhine Riesling

More complex than Cape Riesling, and with more complex flavours, this variety can mature into a fairly oily wine that has a small but loyal market in Europe.

Pinotage

This is actually a hybrid grape variety, created in South Africa by Dr Perold who crossed Pinot Noir with Cinsault back in 1926. The result was Pinotage, characterised by its intense, deep colour and flavours of dark fruits, chocolate and smoky tobacco. It is becoming an increasingly popular addition to the wine market and gaining acclaim in many areas.

KEY WINE PRODUCING AREAS

South African vineyards are divided into regions, districts and wards (with wards being the smallest). In the Cape, there are three main regions which predominate in the export market.

Coastal region

Constantia

- The oldest of the winemaking districts, Constantia faces Table Bay and has a cool maritime climate now producing excellent Sauvignon Blancs and Bordeaux blend reds.

- The Constantia dessert wine which was so popular in 18th and 19th century Europe is once again being produced, with *Klein Constantia* using a variety of Muscat in a sweet blend.

Constantia can legitimately claim to have been Napoleon's favourite dessert wine.

Stellenbosch

- This district is one of the stars of South African production and houses the Oenological Viticultural Research Institute.

- Lies slightly more inland than Constantia with a diverse microclimate. Granite-based soils in the east encourage the production of some excellent reds, whilst the sandstone soils of the west support fine white wine.

- Makes both excellently supple Cabernet Sauvignon and inky black Shiraz, with some Sauvignon Blanc production to complement the ubiquitous Chenin Blanc.

- Notable producers include *Meerlust*, *Waterford Estate* and *Simonsig*.

Boberg region

Paarl

- Home to KMV's main winery and administrative centre, the district is still dominated by a small number of major producers.

- The light soils mean excellent fertility although the district is much hotter than Stellenbosch, limiting genuine quality production to high altitude.

Tulbagh

- The producer *Kanonkop* produces an excellent Pinotage here, packed with blackberry and plum flavour and underwritten by an earthy mouth-feel.

- The undulating terrain has a large mineral content in the gravelly soil and benefits from both abundant sunshine and cooling rainstorms.

Pocket fact 🍷

Historically, the most famous wine to come out of South Africa was Constantia. This legendary dessert wine is even mentioned in Sense & Sensibility, *where it is recommended by Mrs Jennings for 'its healing powers on a disappointed heart'.*

Breede River Valley region

Worcester

- Although not the most fashionable of districts, Worcester is now beginning to produce some real quality amongst its light wines.

- The climate is extreme, often swinging between blazing hot summers and frozen winters.

- This district is also the largest producer of Brandy in South Africa.

One to watch: Kanonkop Estates 🍇

A family-run winery that produces wines of international acclaim. Generally held to be of equal quality to that deemed Premier Cru in French classification.

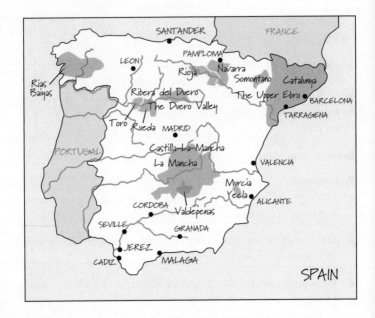

~~~| SPAIN |~~~

HISTORY

Spain has a long tradition of winemaking, and a good selection of indigenous grape varieties, but it is only recently that it has gained any serious acclaim on the global market. This could well be a response to the increasing number of New World wines that the modern consumer is exposed to. These have made the market more open to the rich, fruity, rather exuberant wines that come from warmer climates such as that of Mediterranean Spain.

CLIMATE AND GEOGRAPHY

Spain's warm climate allows grapes to ripen easily and fully, although over-hot summers can occasionally spoil a crop. In 2003 a law was passed sanctioning the irrigation of vineyards, which swiftly solved this minor problem.

GRAPE VARIETIES

Spain is home to an abundance of grape varieties, both international and indigenous, and some of the most commonly grown are listed below.

Red

- Native grapes include Tempranillo and Tinto de Toro.

- Non-indigenous varieties of Cabernet Sauvignon, Merlot and Grenache (Garnacha).

White

- Native varieties of Pedro Ximénez, Verdejo Macabeo, Xarel-lo, Parellada and Palomino Fino.

- International grapes include Chardonnay, Sauvignon Blanc, Gewürztraminer, white Grenache Blanc (Garnacha Blanca) and Muscat (Moscatel).

KEY WINE PRODUCING AREAS

The most noteworthy regions and their produce, at a glance.

The Duero Valley

Toro
With only eight wine estates, this area could easily be overlooked. But as the producer of some of Spain's finest red wines from the fabulously fruity and wonderfully crimson Tinto de Toro grape, it should not be.

For an excellent example of the quality and explosive flavour of Tinto de Toro, try producer *Vega Sicilia*'s legendary *Pintia* wine.

Other good examples come from *Elias Mora* and *Corral de Campanas*.

Ribera del Duero

This area of northern Spain is home to the modern Spanish wine revolution. Grapes are grown high in the mountains where the dryness and brightness of high altitude is reflected in the flavour of the wines. The cool nights typical of mountain terrain also add to the acidity of the wines, giving them a clarity and buoyancy on the tongue.

Tempranillo is the main grape of the region, and makes plummy wines with additional flavours of cherry and occasional hints of mineral. Again, *Vega Sicilia* makes a fine Tempranillo called *Unico*, in which they blend the spicy Spanish grape with the traditional Bordeaux varieties of Cabernet Sauvignon, Merlot and Malbec to create a tantalising wine.

The Upper Ebro

Rioja

Home of the original Spanish fine red wine of the same name. Rioja is made primarily from the Tempranillo grape, which has been macerated longer, aged in oak and then bottled earlier to give the soft, deep, but still fruity flavours associated with the wine.

Rioja divides into three regions: Alavesa, Alta and Baja. Traditional riojas are often blended from grapes of all three regions. The permitted red grape varieties are Tempranillo, Garnacha, Graciano (a low-yield and uncommon grape) and Mazuelo (the French Carignan).

Rioja label classifications

	White wine		Red wine	
	Age of wine	Of which spent in Oak	Age of Wine	Of which spent in Oak
Vina Joven	N/A	N/A	N/A	N/A
Crianza	1 year	6 months	2 years	6 months
Reserva	2 years	6 months	3 years	1 year
Gran Reserva	4 years	6 months	3 years	2 years

Navarra

A good all-round wine region, producing mildly oaked reds that maintain an authentic kick of Spanish fruitiness, from Tempranillo, Cabernet Sauvignon and Merlot.

On the white front, the area of *Corella* has earned a happy reputation for producing *Moscatel de Grano Menudo* from botrytised grapes, and Chardonnays from anywhere in Navarra are lively. A few scrumptious rosés are also produced in the *Baja Montaña* area.

Somontano

As Somontano only became an established wine region in the 1980s, it has still to stabilise its global reputation. That said, early indications suggest that wines from this area are tasty easy-drinkers that will do well on a popular level.

Tempranillo is proving strong, whilst the Chardonnays stand up against many from France and beyond. Finally, it might also be worth trying a bottle of the surprisingly dry and refreshing Gewürztraminer.

Catalunya

The most famous export is the sparkling *Cava* that has ably deputised for Champagne at a lower market level. It is made using the same method as Champagne (see p.8), but from the native Spanish grapes Macabeo, Xarel-lo and Parellada. Occasionally Chardonnay is added to the cava blend, but Pinot Noir only goes in to make Cava Rosado.

There are only really two producers of Cava that you can look out for: arch rivals *Corodníu* and *Freixenet*.

Castilla-La Mancha

La Mancha DO and Valdepeñas DO

This central region is responsible for almost half of Spain's output, focusing on mostly cooperative-made wines made for drinking young. Valdepeñas is the undulating nook surrounding the southerly town of the same name, making quality red from Tempranillo aged in oak.

Pocket fact ♀

Castilla-La Mancha is home to the most-grown grape variety in the world — Airén. Although seldom seen outside Spain, the wine is sold to the domestic market and also used to make Brandy and constitutes a staggering 30% of Spain's vines.

Yecla DO

In the region of Murcia, this small town is beginning to make a big name for itself in Spanish winemaking. A continental climate has allowed Garnacha and Monastrell to be grown to create supple wines rich with dark berry fruit, enriched with American oak aging and a sense of spiciness.

One to watch: Abadia Retuerta 🍇

Recently founded but unbelievably successful in its short time. Abadia Retuerta produces sumptuous reds in the Ribera del Duero using state of the art technology to maintain every aspect of the winemaking process from humidity during growth to barrel aging.

~~{ USA }~~

HISTORY

Americans have been making wine for several centuries, commencing in the 1560s when the French Huguenot settlers attempted to harvest the native grapes for wine. Unfortunately, the taste of these varieties was not too palatable, and it was not until Franciscan monks began planting European grapes in California that winemaking really began in earnest. After *Phylloxera*, specifically, grafted vines became the norm (see p.xii) and this encouraged the growth of the noble varieties we see today.

Pocket fact ♀

The actor Johnny Depp now has a tattoo that reads Wino Forever (this was altered from Winona Forever after his relationship with Winona Ryder ended).

CLIMATE AND GEOGRAPHY

Being such a vast area of land, the climate and geographical aspect of certain states within America proved highly receptive to vine cultivation.

Parts of California, with its moderating mountains, Mediterranean climate and fertile soils proved to be the most successful region in which to propagate wines. Cooler, northern states such as Oregon and Washington (which share a climate similar to that of Bordeaux) proved excellent for producing some quite remarkable red wines. And finally, white wines found their

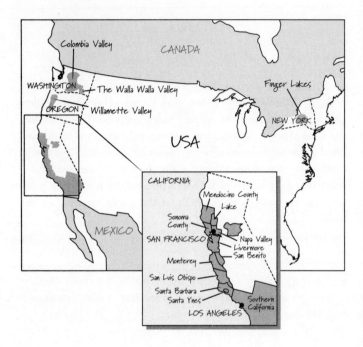

niche in the state of New York where the cooler climate created by inland lakes facilitated the creation of lovely Riesling and Chardonnay.

GRAPE VARIETIES

The sheer scale of America, with its diverse geographical features and wide latitudinal reach, has allowed a vast number of grapes to be cultivated. The most popular and successful of these are listed below.

Red

Cabernet Sauvignon, Merlot, Pinot Noir, and Zinfandel.

White

Chardonnay, Riesling, Sauvignon Blanc.

KEY WINE PRODUCING AREAS

The USA is home to a number of wine producing states, spread right across the continent, but so far only four have really achieved wines of note.

California

Indisputably the homeland of American wine, making over 90% of all American wine. One common climatic feature is extremely hot and dry summers, which necessitate the use of irrigation. The finest regions enjoy cool winters and morning mists.

Napa Valley

- Cool morning mists in this region north of San Francisco encourage the growth of quality wines.

- Cabernet Sauvignon is the most distinguished grape of the Napa Valley, creating some of the world's most successful wines.

- Acclaim for Napa Valley wines came overnight when a Cabernet Sauvignon from the previously unheard of winery, *Stags Leap Wine Cellars*, came first in a prestigious Parisian tasting in 1976. Thirty years later this winery repeated this victory, and it now lays claim to producing the best Cabernet Sauvignons in the region, and arguably the world.

- Oakville and Rutherford, within the Valley, also produce notable Cabernet Sauvignons.

- Napa Valley Chardonnay is also excellent, producing beauti-fully balanced world-class whites. Delicate, with subtle multi-layered fruit these wines are stunningly evocative. *Grgich Hills* is home to the winemaker that beat Burgundy in 1976, and *Stag's Leap* produces excellent Chardonnay from its *Carneros* vineyard.

Pocket fact 🍷

Director Francis Ford Coppolla described the 1941 Inglenook Cabernet Sauvignon from the Napa as 'one of the finest wines he'd ever tasted'. The bottle which finished fermentation as the Japanese attacked Pearl Harbour cost a cool $24,675 at auction.

Sonoma County

- The origins of wine production in California lie in this region where, back in 1832, some dedicated Franciscan monks started to plant vines.

- Nowadays, Sonoma is celebrated for its excellent Chardonnays that have good aging potential. *Landmark Vineyard* and *Sonoma-Cutrer's Les Pierres* vineyard make particularly delicious wines.

- Pinot Noir (from wineries such as *Hudson*, *Sangiacomo* and *Truchard*) is growing in quality and popularity, whilst Cabernet Franc, Syrah and Merlot from this region can also be very good.

- *Ridge Vineyards* produces some of the very best wine in the USA – its Cabernet Sauvignon was another of the high scorers at the Judgement of Paris and they remain world class.

Mendocino County

- Connected to Sonoma by the Russian River, this northern region is a somewhat cooler extension of its southern neighbour.

- Perhaps best suited to fresh varietals such as Chardonnay, Sauvignon Blanc and Cabernet Sauvignon.

- This region is also a centre for organic wines, with leading producers such as *Bonterra* responsible for excellent output.

Pocket fact 🍷

Before Prohibition, North Carolina was the USA's top wine producer by volume. Nowadays it is almost unheard of in the wine world.

Washington State

It is not surprising that this state, which occupies a latitude perfectly between that of Bordeaux and Burgundy, has a reputation for producing fine wines and is the second biggest wine-growing state of the USA. It's best known for Pinot Noir.

Colombia Valley

Washington's oldest wine-growing region, and also its coolest, allowing it to produce the occasional remarkable Chardonnay. More recently, Syrah has been taking centre stage, and that from the *Red Willow* vineyard is particularly good.

The Walla Walla Valley

A good place to look if you want to sample a bold Merlot or Cabernet Sauvignon from America. Colombia Gorge is famed for aromatic Chardonnay and rich, aromatic Zinfandel.

Willamette Valley

This unassuming corner of Oregon rose to fame in the 1960s when David Letts planned Pinot Noir in his *Eyrie Vineyards* to great effect. Since then, the Willamette Valley has been known for producing superior wines from this grape.

Pinot Noirs from this area are softer and fruitier than their European counterparts. For a sophisticated drink try a wine from the *Domaine Drouhin*, and for something a little more vibrant the *Beaux Frères* winery should suit.

Pocket fact 🍷

Well-known American producers Ernest and Julio Gallo's wine empire started from very humble origins. Needing to kick start their business but with no idea how to make wine, they turned to their local library for help and got out a book on winemaking. From this simple guide they learnt the principles of the process, and began to build their empire, now one of the world's largest wine producers.

New York

Although this is America's third most important wine-growing state, around two-thirds of the wineries in New York are less than 15 years old and very small scale establishments. Nonetheless, they are ambitious and dedicated, resulting in high-quality wines beginning to creep into the international market from this state.

Finger Lakes

Wineries such as *Red Newt* and *Standing Stone* are creating excellent Riesling and Chardonnay in a continental climate created by the surrounding lakes.

One to watch:
Stag's Leap Wine Cellars 🍇

One of the founding fathers of Californian winemaking, this vineyard carries on a tradition of selecting and picking only the very ripest grapes from the vines in order to create wines with unique combinations of big flavours that drink softly.

4

ENJOYING WINE

⊶ WINE TASTING ⊷

The title of this section is actually slightly misleading as a more accurate name would be 'Wine Smelling'. Appreciating wine and understanding its depth actually comes down to the sense of smell as opposed to that of taste, so bear in mind when you start tasting to pay attention to your nose as well as your mouth.

The steps below take you through a sensible approach to tasting wine.

STEP ONE: LOOK AT THE WINE

You can tell a lot about a wine from its appearance, and there are three things to look out for.

Colour

Red wine

- The colour of a red wine will give you a good clue as to the age of the wine in your glass. Young red wines tend to start off with rich, deep colours that lessen with age (as the tannins work their magic – see p.4) With a few years of aging, red wines will turn more tawny in colour (like the burnt light red of a brick) so the lighter the red in your glass, the older it is.

- The colour of the wine can also give you a hint as to which grape varieties have been used in the wine. Pinot Noir will always make a fairly pale red wine, whereas other varieties are expected to be almost black.

White wine

- As white wine ages it acquires a deeper hue (due to the slight oxidisation which occurs in aging vessels). Wines will start off pale, sometimes lemon, sometimes light gold, in colour and then deepen to rich golden ambers as aging progresses.

- As with red, you can take a good guess at the grapes used in a white wine by the way it looks. Cool climate wines always tend to be less coloured than their warmer counterparts even when the grape variety used is the same. Riesling in particular is notable for its delicate, almost greenish hue.

Legs

This is the term given to the droplets of colourless liquid that run down the inside of the glass after swirling, as the alcohol content of the wine is momentarily separated by surface tension. They are an indication of alcohol content and allow the experienced taster to gauge the alcohol content of a wine blind, by judging how pronounced they are. In France, legs are referred to as 'tears'.

Bead

This name refers to the size of the bubbles in sparkling wine. Generally speaking, Champagne has a finer bead than other sparkling wines so look out for that at parties so you can tell if you are being fobbed off with a cheap alternative!

STEP TWO: SMELL THE WINE

This is the most important step in the tasting process, as the aroma of wine will tell you all about the grapes used, the aging process behind the wine, and what you can expect it to taste like.

1) Swirl the glass

Before you start, make sure that you are holding your glass by the stem and not the bowl. It might feel a little precarious at first but it actually gives you greater control over the swirl (which you will need!)

Be a little careful; you want to give it a confident swill without any wine actually making it out of the glass.

Only fill your glass around an eighth full to swirl it, and then just do a couple of loose, circular movements with the wrist and watch as the wine laps the side of the glass. This action serves to agitate the wine and increase the surface area that gains contact with the air, helping to release the full range of aromas.

2) Have a sniff

Take a gentle smell, increasing the intensity as you encounter the aromas of the wine. This gradual approach ensures that you don't spoil your senses in the case of a faulty wine.

Remember that these aromas will generally fall into two categories: young wines will only have *primary aromas* which are all fruit based whether a blackcurrant red or a peachy white; older wines will have *secondary aromas* as well as the fruity notes, and these are often more earthy – wood or tobacco for example.

STEP THREE: TASTE THE WINE

Your first taste of wine should be a little sip. Move it around your mouth so it hits all areas, and then just hold it in there for a few seconds whilst you purse your lips and draw air over the wine. This gives time for the flavours to develop in contact with the air.

There are two areas that you need to focus on once the wine is finally on your tongue:

- **The flavours that hit your taste buds**

  Initially, you will probably be hit by one distinct flavour, and this is known as the *forepalate*. But swiftly following this initial reaction will be a further two taste revelations, the *midpalate* and the *endpalate*. So, whilst the wine is in your mouth, you are looking to experience three waves of taste impression if possible.

- **The aromas you can smell**

  Whilst you are getting to grips with the effect that the wine is having in your mouth, you must also take notice of what is happening in your nose.

  Aromas from the wine in your mouth will seep up into your nasal canal and create sensations in the receptors there that actually give you the true 'taste' of the wine. (NB The reason you can't taste food when you have a cold is because these receptors are blocked.) To make the most of their power, breathe in and out through your nose as you taste the wine, and draw a little more air in through the mouth to maximise the aromas coming off the wine into the nose.

Weight/tannins/acidity

Acidity will affect the sides of your tongue towards the rear, making your mouth water slightly. You'll want to see this in a fresh, white wine but not necessarily in a powerful red. Tannins have a drying effect on the gums and tongue, unlike acidity, and are an important aspect of a wine's potential to age. These will most likely be noticed in red wines. Weight can also be described as 'Body' or 'Mouth-feel'. This quite simply applies to how heavy a wine feels in your mouth — a light one is described as light-bodied and heavy as full-bodied.

STEP FOUR: SPIT

This is perhaps the most important piece of advice if you are tasting a multitude of wines. Drinking every wine proffered is likely to lead (unsurprisingly) to intoxication, which is clearly unhelpful in the context of an analytical tasting. Likewise, swallowing tasting measures is likely to tire your palate and make it more difficult to detect and appreciate differing flavours.

STEP FIVE: THE FINISH

Take note of the final flavours that linger in your mouth once the wine has left it. These may well be different to those that you tasted whilst it was in your mouth. This aftertaste of the wine is called the *length*, and generally speaking the longer lasting the length the better quality the wine.

Pocket tip 🍇

Keep a journal in which to jot down all the wines that you taste and your impressions of each. This will not only help you identify characteristics and develop the subtlety of your description of them, but also provide you with a useful record of which wines to buy again and which to avoid.

⊣ WINE TASTING ETIQUETTE ⊢

- **Hold the glass by the stem**
  Don't grasp the glass around the bulb at the top, but instead hold the stem about three quarters of the way up. As mentioned previously, this will make it easier for you to swirl your glass with grace, and avoid your wine heating up as you clasp it in your hand. It also ensures the nose of the wine is not confused by any residual odour from your hands.

- **Don't wear white if you are tasting red**
  Common sense, and better safe than sorry if you're going to be doing a lot of swirling...

- **Know when to spit**
  If you are sampling several different bottles then it is something of a necessity to ensure you don't have to be carried out at the end of the night.

At most large wine tastings there will be a receptacle or two for depositing your mouthful of wine once you have appreciated its flavours to the full. It's a pretty standard part of wine tastings, and if you're a novice, you'll soon get used to it.

⊶| HOW TO DESCRIBE |⊷
WHAT YOU TASTE

'Wine is bottled poetry.'
Robert Louis Stevenson

Verbalising the wine tasting experience can be difficult. There is a fine line between sounding competent and sounding pretentious, but with the use of the common and accepted phrases listed below, you can describe wines fairly easily.

Pocket tip 🍇
Remember you can never really say anything too wrong at a wine tasting because at the end of the day enjoyment comes down to personal preference.
  Do remember that flavours are not representative of actual fruit in the wine but simply what the wine is evocative of.

Common terms

Acetic	Never something you want to find in a wine at a tasting as this basically means it tastes like vinegar.
Acidic	If a wine tastes a bit sharp it can have high acidity.
Ageworthy	Applies to wines that would benefit from a bit more aging. In red wines this applies to those which are still a bit strong on the tannin front (creating that dry, astringent taste in the mouth), and in whites when they are still a bit sweet or acidic.
Aggressive	Any wine that assaults the senses with excess acid or tannin.
Ample	Wines that feel full and bountiful in your mouth.
Aromatic	This describes a particularly perfumed fruit character in the wine.
Astringent	Describes the dry, almost rough feeling that some wines can leave in the mouth as a result of high tannins.
Austere	A wine that leaves you with the feeling described above.
Balanced/rounded	When there are no dominant flavours to the wine (such as acidity, fruit, sugar, etc) and the flavours interact harmoniously, it is said to be balanced or rounded.
Big	For that wine that makes a big impression. Can apply to it being full-bodied, flavoursome or intensely aromatic.
Body	A very important and familiar term. Wines can be light, medium or full-bodied depending on the amount of alcohol and extracts contained in the wine, which you can feel weighing in upon your tongue. This is one of the principal characteristics of a wine and should be of especial note.
Bold	Wines with distinctive aromas and flavours that are easily identifiable as separate components.
Bouquet	Describes a complex array of aromas on the nose.
Buttery	A rounded smell and taste often imbued into oak-aged wines.
Character	Just like humans, the character of a wine refers to its personality and integrity. An abstract concept that relies on a thorough tasting.

Common terms

Clean	A wine that doesn't overly grate or linger on the palate.
Complex	A wine that has many aromas and flavours weaving around one another. Complexity is easy to spot if you get a combination of primary, fruity aromas and secondary flavours such as vanilla, wood or spice.
Cooked	Not a flattering description. Refers to a wine that has a prunish flavour resulting from excessive heat in the fermentation stage.
Crisp	Applied to wines with a good level of acidity that gives a light, fresh flavour in the mouth.
Deep	This can describe a particular richness in the taste of a wine.
Dull	As it sounds, a lack lustre wine with no distinguishable features or style.
Earthy	The aroma or flavour of damp earth has an inviting rustic quality.
Firm	A balanced wine with well-defined flavours.
Flabby	The opposite of firm; usually applies to wines with low acidity levels that are left sticky and cloyingly sweet.
Fleshy	This would be used on a wine that feels robust and solid in the mouth (usually due to a high concentration of fruit extract).
Fruity	Self-explanatory. Look for strong, pleasing fruit flavours including apples, berries, citrus, peaches, pears, etc.
Grassy	Only relevant to white wine and is quite literally the taste and aroma of that wonderful smell of freshly cut grass. Can also be referred to as *capsicum*, *gooseberry* or *lime zest*.
Green	Describes a freshness in white wine or immaturity in reds.
Heavy	Really a measurement of the body of the wine.
Lean/stringy/thin	High acidity and low flavour makes a wine all these things, and not much fun to drink.
Meaty	Some red wines exhibit a distinctive savoury or gamey taste, such as those from the Mourvèdre grape.

(continued)

Common terms

Mineral	When a wine tastes slightly of rock or stone. Usually balanced against acidity, this is common in New Zealand Sauvignon Blanc and Burgundian Chardonnays.
Nose	Describes the set of flavours that distinguish the smell of the wine.
Nutty	An aroma distinguishable in some nicely aged whites.
Oaky	As the name suggests, flavours that are created by aging in oak barrels. Look out for vanilla, buttery, smokey and even tobacco aromas and tastes.
Petrol	A positive trait in some aromatic varietals.
Racy	Wines that are zippy on the tongue because of pleasantly high acidity.
Smooth/soft	Can be applied to red wines with relatively low tannin levels (such as Merlot), or low acidity whites that are mellow in the mouth.
Spicy	Use whenever you get a whiff of cinnamon, cloves, pepper or any other exotic spice flavour you can think of.
Tannic	Although tannins are associated with dryness in the mouth, they are also associated with richness of flavour and depth of colour. Because of this, applying the description *tannic* to a wine is not bad if this element is balanced by strong fruitiness.

Pocket tip

Aromatic grape varieties include Gewürztraminer, Muscat, Riesling and Sauvignon Blanc.

Most common bottles

Bordeaux	Straight-sided with high, steep shoulders. Usually made from dark green glass for red wines, light green for white and clear for dessert. This, in many ways, is the most common bottle.

Most common bottles

Burgundy	Shallow, slope-shouldered, rounded bottle used for both reds and whites. Made from light green or clear glass.
Flute d'Alsace	Alsace wines are sold in tall, slender, green bottles similar to those used in Germany for wines produced in the Mosel and Rhine regions. To distinguish the two German wines, the Mosel bottles are bright green whilst the Rhine bottles are brown.
	This elegant, slim bottle is also used for varieties around the world including Riesling, Gewürztraminer and Pinot Gris.
Bocksbeutel	This bottle is used for wines from the Franconia region of Germany and also some Portuguese wines (where it is called Cantil). It is a squashed ellipsoid shape – flattened and round.
Champagne	There is no mistaking a Champagne bottle. Although it is just a variation on the Burgundy design, it is made from much sturdier glass from that used for bottles for still wine and is topped off by the requisite mushroom cork and wire hat combo.

Pocket fact ♀

The Champagne bottle has to be strong enough to withstand six atmospheres of pressure to ensure it doesn't burst under the strain of the bubbles within.

How to tell if a wine is corked

If you're in any doubt about recognising if a wine is corked, don't worry – you will be able to tell something is wrong immediately.

Here's the science

A wine becomes corked when it has been in contact with a cork that is infected by a fungus that produces the chemical

1,2,4-trichloroanisole (TCA to those in the know). It is this chemical that gives a corked wine its distinctly unpleasant aroma and taste.

Telltale signs that a wine is corked

*A corked wine is **not** one that has bits of cork floating in it. That is usually just an accident on opening and has no effect on the wine inside.*

Corked wine is distinctive in its unpleasantness, both smelling and tasting of a mixture of mould, mushrooms and smelly socks. If you are getting these aromas when you swill your wine, the best thing to do is pour it down the sink.

Unfortunately, there is little way of avoiding accidentally buying a corked wine although many retailers will now exchange the bottle for you. It is a relatively irregular fault which it is important not to over-stress.

'The best use of bad wine is to drive away poor relations.'
French proverb

⊷ SERVING SUGGESTIONS ⊶

'Here's to the corkscrew — a useful key to unlock the storehouse of wit, the treasury of laughter, the front door of fellowship, and the gate of pleasant folly.'
WEP French

Although there are quite a few rules to remember when it comes to serving a wine, they can all be broken down into bite-sized slices of information that are easy to digest.

HOW TO OPEN A BOTTLE OF WINE

The frustration of pulling out only half a cork, or breaking your corkscrew leaving both cork and screw wedged inside the bottle, is all too common. But these catastrophes are also easily avoidable...

Choose the right corkscrew

Too many a wine-opening crisis could have been avoided if a sensible corkscrew had been used in the first place. There are many types of corkscrew gadgets and gizmos available on the market, but for cost-effective varieties that work look no further than either of the following:

The winged corkscrew

Simple but effective. Place the circular rim of the corkscrew over the lip of the bottle and the wings will rise higher and higher as you turn the screw into the cork. Once the wings are nice and high, pull them down and out pops the cork – easy.

The waiter's corkscrew

A slim and comfortable corkscrew that is just as easy to use but just ever so slightly more stylish than the winged variety described above. It comes with a knife to remove the foil from the top of the bottle first, then simply screw in the device and use the side lever to apply pressure to the lip of the bottle as you ease the cork out. Some side levers are hinged in the middle to help you ease the cork out in two stages.

Pocket tip 🍇

No matter which style of corkscrew you use, always make sure that you purchase one in which the screw forms a proper helix, as opposed to consisting of a spiral attached to a straight central core. These grip the cork much more effectively, ensuring that you run far less risk of getting left with half a cork in your vino.

Opening still wine

- Always remove the top section of the foil around the tip of the bottle, ideally using a foil-cutter.

- Insert the point of the corkscrew into the centre of the cork and gently twist down in a straight line. It is vital not to veer off at an angle when screwing into the cork as this is a sure fire way of causing the cork to break when you try to pull it out.

Pocket tip 🍇

Don't twist the corkscrew all the way through the bottom of the cork, as then you risk dropping little shavings from the centre of the cork into the wine as they are pushed out by the corkscrew.

- If you are using a winged corkscrew you can simply pull the wings down at this point and the cork should pop out whole. If you are using a waiter's friend, rest the lever on the lip of the bottle and hold it in place with your hand to ensure it doesn't slip, then gently lift up the other end of the corkscrew and coax out the cork.

What to do if the cork has snapped

Even with the right corkscrew and technique this problem occurs, most commonly, at the most inopportune moment, such as when opening a bottle in front of guests at the table. But it's easily rectified.

The best way

The easiest, although not the most aesthetically pleasing solution to this problem is simply to drive the remaining section of cork into the wine bottle, then decant off the wine into a separate vessel. An effective tool for forcing the cork down the neck and into the body of the wine is a wooden spoon: sturdy and without the risk of injury.

The rest

If you really can't bring yourself to actively force a cork into your wine, there are a couple of other options open to you:

1) Invest in a device for removing broken corks – there are a number of these on the market although they rarely prove a cost-effective solution to this very occasional problem.

2) Sometimes it is possible to carefully insert your corkscrew into the broken remainder of the cork and ease it out. Be warned though: only try this if a considerable amount of cork is left in the bottle as otherwise you run the risk of it crumbling in its entirety into the wine below, which you will then have to sieve before serving...

Opening Champagne and sparkling wines

Whilst it would be nice to imitate a Grand Prix winner and let the cork fly from the bottle so a jet of vintage Champagne sprays your guests, this is an impractical and expensive way of opening bubbly.

Instead, do remember 'safety first' when opening a bottle of fizz, and aim for a controlled pop with the drink remaining within the bottle ready for pouring.

- Place your thumb over the top of the cork and make sure the bottle is pointing in a safe direction: away from the dog, the lights, the windows and any friends or relatives who are nearby.

- Take your thumb off the cork to undo the wire cage over the cork and remove it, then quickly pop your thumb back on just in case the cork decides to prematurely escape.

- Hold the bottle at a 45° angle and grasp the top of the cork that is protruding from the bottle with one hand, using the other to slowly turn the bottle to ease it out. ALWAYS remember to twist the bottle and not the cork to avoid a deafening pop and an out of control cork flying around your living room.

• As you twist the bottle, you will feel pressure building as the cork loosens, so keep a tight grip on it and let it gently ease out with a soft fizz, which will preserve both wine and bubbles from getting lost in the opening process.

Sabrage

Opening Champagne with a sword may seem dangerous but it is spectacular and relatively safe. This tradition, purportedly started by Napoleon's troops trying to impress a lady aristocrat, is perhaps best left to the professionals of La Confrérie du Sabre d'Or. There are many tutors and it is an exciting skill to learn: a sword is used to strike an area at the neck of the bottle which represents a natural weak point and the pressure of the liquid encourages the cork to fire off dramatically. The ultimate opening!

WHAT TO SERVE YOUR WINE IN

Red, white, rosé, sparkling and fortified wines all benefit from being placed in glasses designed to show these wines off at their best.

Red wine

Glasses for red wine have a large bowl that allows the maximum exposure of wine to the air in order to allow the aromas to escape.

Full-bodied red wines, such as Cabernet Sauvignon, are usually served in *Bordeaux glasses* which have a wide opening at the rim.

Fruity reds, such as Pinot Noir, are served in *Burgundy glasses* that have a slimmer, tapered opening at the rim so the rich scents don't overpower the drinking experience.

White wine

Traditionally this glass will have a smaller bowl, longer stem and narrower base than that used for red wine. The longer stem by which to hold the glass, and the smaller surface area of the bowl, work together to reduce heat transfer between the wine and the hand, so your white wine will stay cooler for longer.

Rosé wine

Similar to a white wine glass but generally slightly smaller with a wider bowl. This style can also be used for sweet wines and aperitifs.

Champagne

Champagne flutes should be tall and slim to retain as much of the bubbly carbon dioxide as possible and ensure the finest bead for as long as possible.

> *Pocket fact*
>
> *The first Champagne flutes were modelled around the shape of Cleopatra's breast, but in recent years these shallow, bowl-shaped flutes have gone out of favour as they cause the contents to go flat far quicker than the narrower variety.*

Fortified wine

There is no real consensus as to what makes the perfect glass from which to sip fortified wines. As a general rule it should be smaller than that used for any other wine, and never more than half-full to avoid the odours of the alcohol content from overpowering the aromas of the wine itself.

How full to fill your glass?

The general rule is that glasses should be filled between a third to half-full, allowing the recipient to swirl their glass without spilling. Full glasses may seem generous, but impede the enjoyment of a wine.

THE TABLE OF TEMPERATURES

A warm white on a sunny day is never appreciated, and serving a chilled red will deeply affect its flavour. If in doubt, refer to this handy table below to make sure your wines are perfect every time.

Type of wine	Serving temperature range (°C)	Optimum serving temperature (°C)
White	4–10	8
Sparkling	6–10	8
Old World red	14–18	17
New World red	16–19	18
Sweet/dessert	4–8	6
Fortified	14–18	16

NB: Some wines operate as exceptions and very light reds such as Beaujolais may benefit from a very light chilling.

POURING WINE

There is a charming Victorian adage that states one should 'hold a woman by the waist and a bottle by the neck'. Although there is undoubted wisdom in such a statement, judging by the pouring methods of waiters around the world this isn't how it's done.

The rules that apply to a good wine waiter in a restaurant are also a good set to abide by when serving wine to dinner party guests.

• You should always hold a wine bottle at the bottom and in the palm of your hand, popping your thumb into the *punt* (small dent) in the bottom for added stability when pouring.

- Pour a sample – to test it is essential. This is the final point at which you can find out if your wine is corked before accepting the bottle and serving the wine to all your guests.

- Serve the wine to guests by moving clockwise around the table. The proper etiquette is to stand at their right hand shoulder (ladies first is optional).

Pocket tip 🍇

Pour the wine very slowly to prevent it splashing and slopping out of the glass onto your clean tablecloth. When you finish serving each guest, give the bottle a little twist before lifting it away from the glass as this will stop it dripping.

Pouring aids

The cheat's trick to pouring the perfect glass of wine with no slops, spills or drips. The most effective on the market are little metallic discs that you roll into the top of your bottle for a faultless pour every time.

Champagne and sparkling wine should be poured slowly to ensure a languid flow which prevents too much fizz and an overflowing glass. These bubbles are created by the speed with which the liquid hits the glass. If pouring for a large group, try 'charging' the glasses first by adding a small amount of Champagne to each. This should allow an easy pour with no need to revisit glasses.

Does a wine need to breathe?

It is not essential to let a wine breathe, although it can aid some wines with particularly robust tannins. Youthful wines

> *may be relieved of any aggressive bite and encouraged to display some more complex aromas than they otherwise would.*
>
> *If you are going to let your wine breathe, it will benefit from being decanted into a vessel that is specifically designed to maximise the interaction between the wine and the air.*

DECANTING

You will have undoubtedly seen exceptionally ornate decanters before if not, in fact, used or acquired one. They are intended as an alternative vessel from which to pour the wine, allowing for any sediment cast during bottle aging to be removed before drinking. Decanting will also allow the wine to breathe, by exposing a large volume to air during the pouring.

Generally, inexpensive wine bought off the shelf will not need decanting, although may benefit from the aeration. Most bottle-aged reds will cast some sediment, however, and there is an established method in order to avoid this ending up in your glass. Remove the entire foil capsule from the neck of the bottle, then open the bottle as normal. Whilst holding a small light source behind the neck of the bottle, carefully pour into a decanter (or other suitable vessel such as a carafe) whilst observing the flow from the neck. When you see sediment beginning to follow the wine, stop pouring and set aside the half-glass or so of sediment-laden wine. This by-product can be used very successfully in cooking as adding it to sauce or gravy will demonstrate. The decanted wine can itself now be poured and enjoyed as normal.

5

WINE AND FOOD

Wine is largely drunk when accompanying a meal, therefore it is important to ensure that the enjoyment of both is maximised by your choice of wine.

⊶ PAIRING WINE WITH FOOD ⊷

Pairing wine with food need not be a complicated process. Drinking wine from the same origin as your food is often the best indicator of a match. Nothing goes with Languedocien Cassoulet like a Corbières, for example.

One can, however, take a more scientific approach and examine the differing flavours present within wine and food to try to create a harmonic balance of flavour profiles.

'It is better for pearls to pass through the lips of swine than good wine to pass through the lips of the indifferent.'
Mark Luedtke

BASIC FLAVOUR PROFILES

The easiest way to match food with wine is to note whether your dish is predominantly sweet, acid or bitter and choose a wine with the same characteristics.

This general guideline explains why sweet wines are served with desserts, and why tannic red wines that are slightly bitter work best with steak; but what constitutes an 'acidic' meal? Of course, you will never be confronted with a plate of lemons to which you will have to match a wine, but if you would consider squeezing a lemon onto your dish (as in the case of seafood) then it would be classed as acidic. In these instances, a white wine with high acidity is the best pairing.

Keeping these rules in mind, food and wine pairing is an essentially individual endeavour. Different people swear by odd combinations that can make their meal yet would put others off. Listed below are suggestions for you to try, although remember that they are by no means comprehensive. Exploring the interaction of these flavours is both a noble and enjoyable exercise, as well as an excellent basis for discussion with friends.

Fish

The most common pairing is a fish dish with a light, acidic white wine, but it is by no means your only option; Champagne and sparkling wines are also considered classic accompaniments. If you are partaking of a flavourful, Mediterranean style main then a rosé might be the wine for you; alternatively, there is nothing to stop you complementing a meaty tuna steak with a tasty little red number.

Fish	Wine
Cod, sole, plaice, haddock	These go well with fairly rich white wines including Burgundys, New World Chardonnays, white Hermitage, Pinot Gris and dry Rieslings.
Crab, lobster	If you are having crab or lobster choose a rich New World Chardonnay, white Rioja or Meursault.
Bass, sea perch	Goes with any good white wine; Burgundy, Soave or Viognier would be ideal.
Monkfish	A substantial fish that can stand up to an aged wine with more complex flavours such as white Burgundy or white Rhône. It will also cope well with a red such as Merlot.

Fish	Wine
Salmon	With this rich, oily fish you can opt for a white or a red wine. The best whites are those from the Loire Valley or good-quality Chardonnays, although a splash of pink Champagne or a Provençal rosé can work rather nicely as well! On the red front, a young, light Pinot Noir or Sancerre would be great.
Smoked salmon	If your salmon is smoked you need to consider a different batch of wines as an accompaniment. Champagne is the classic, but Premier Cru Chablis, Gewürztraminer and even a dry rosé can be equally complementary.
Bouillabaisse (fish soup)	Try Provençal rosés, white Châteauneuf-du-Pape or Soave.
Swordfish	Works best with Languedoc whites, such as Picpoul de Pinet, Chardonnay or Sauvignon Blanc.
Tuna	A meaty fish that can take almost any white wine and a few reds. Try flavourful whites such as New World Chardonnays, or a full-bodied red from any region.

Red meat

Red meats stick to kind by preferring to partner wines that are red in colour, but different cooking styles allow for a veritable cacophony of flavour combinations. For example, a traditional beef roast will benefit from a complex, aged red wine, whereas a spicy curry dish will prefer a simple but fruity youngster as a companion. So read on and explore the dangerous liaisons between red meat and wine that will put the bite back into your dinner.

Meat	Wine
Steak	Works best with big reds whose tannins stand up to the meat. Think peppery Shiraz or the herbal notes of Southern French blockbusters such as Châteauneuf-du-Pape. Riojas also combine an excellent interplay of oak and vanilla, which complements the flavours of a good steak.

(continued)

Meat	Wine
Stewed beef	Full-bodied reds work best: Burgundy, St Emilion, Rhône, Australian Shiraz.
Roast beef	Quite simply the most expensive, complex, mature red you can afford. A quality Cabernet Sauvignon or Super Tuscan.
Beef stroganoff	An extremely full-bodied red such as Châteauneuf-du-Pape, Valpolicella or a good Californian Zinfandel.
Black pudding, sausages	Not exactly gourmet items, but nonetheless worthy of being washed down by a good red. Something gutsy from Australia, Languedoc or the Rhône should do the trick.
Burgers	Usually served with salad and tomato, which pits meaty flavours against a fresher taste. Try a buxom Californian Cabernet Sauvignon to balance rich dense fruit against mid-bodied freshness.
Cold meats	A Bordeaux or Burgundy should complement most cold cuts of red meat. For salamis and chorizos, try a fruity yet firm Zinfandel or Barbera.
Haggis	The oaty, earthy flavour of the haggis works best with a young Pouilly-Fuissé or rich Rhône.
Gammon, ham	A Pinot Blanc from any region works well, although a Chablis is also an excellent choice as the roundness of the Chardonnay complements the salty, richness of the ham.
Pork	The most versatile of our coloured meats, as it suits Pinot Gris or Gewürztraminer white wines, and Chianti, Rioja and Médoc reds.
Lamb	This is best suited to the complicated reds that add to the experience; Chianti, Rioja, Médoc and St Emilion. Red Burgundy is also recommended as it is lighter than Cabernet Sauvignon, which works better with the lighter meat.
Liver, bacon	Works best with young, quality reds including Beaujolais, Californian Merlots and Argentinean Malbec.
Spaghetti bolognese, cannelloni, meatballs, etc.	Italian dishes need Italian reds; Valpolicella or Chianti are ideal, as their zesty yet powerfully fruity characters carry off the herbs and richness of these dishes. Zinfandel is another food-friendly wine with enough fruit and body to carry off Italian meals.

Meat	Wine
Traditional pies	Choose a hearty red for such a traditional English meal. Châteauneuf-du-Pape, Claret, Shiraz and Côtes-du-Rhône all make for a winning combination.

Fowl

Fowl encompasses a good variety of styles of meat making it a surprisingly versatile category when it comes to experimenting with wine pairing.

Fowl	Wine
Chicken, guinea fowl	Traditionally paired with classic whites such as Pinot Gris, dry Riesling and white Burgundy. But roasted they also provide a surprisingly good foil for a red Burgundy as well.
Coq au vin	A creamy New World Chardonnay or lively young Beaujolais will be perfect. Also try a Chilean Carmenère for a darker flavour.
Duck, goose	Rich, fatty birds require robust, flavourful wines. Treat your senses and combine with a red or white Hermitage, a heavy hitting white from Burgundy, St Emilion or Pomerol.
Quail	Takes red Burgundy and Pinot Noir very well.
Turkey	With its tendency to dryness, this bird is best matched with a fruity Beaujolais, Côtes-du-Rhône, or red Zinfandel. Alternatively, stick to white, with a big rich Californian or Burgundian Chardonnay. Red Burgundy is also often suggested for Christmas.
Foie gras	A controversial food to match. Sauternes and Barsac are the most obvious recourse, but some favour a characterful red such as Amarone to cut through the fat and be softened by the foie gras. Port is also a common pairing for its concentrated, almost sweet fruit. Try goose foie gras with the sweet whites and duck with the reds.

Game

Probably the least explored food group, which contains some of the most complex, dark flavours that can be perfectly exploited by coupling them with an equally mysterious wine.

Game	Wine
Pheasant, grouse, partridge, wood cock	A mature and full-bodied red which can stand up to rich flavours in the meat such as Burgundy, St Emilion, Pomerol, Rioja, Chianti or Languedoc.
Rabbit	Brilliant with a Burgundy, and also with some of the rustic reds of the Languedoc where fruit and body is matched with a herbal note.
Venison, wild boar	A big strong deer or, if you are adventurous, wild boar deserve nothing less than a block-buster red. Valpolicella, Châteauneuf-du-Pape, St Emilion, and Chianti or Pinotage are ideal matches to the lush flavours on show.

Exotic spicy food

It can sometimes be difficult to match wines with exotic world cuisine, as they have often developed in isolation of each other. It may seem churlish to pair wines with the entire culinary output of a nation, yet these are intended as basic guidelines to help you to arrive at a complementary choice.

Region	Wine
Thai food	Thai food is often characterised by aromatic spiciness and the presence of ingredients such as lemongrass. Try experimenting with Rieslings, particularly from Alsace, as this will complement the aromatic nature of both food and wine.
Indian curries	Depending on the spice of a curry, it is possible to find often slightly sweet acidic varieties that work well. Try German Gewürztraminer or Riesling – the light aromatic sweetness can complement spice, whereas firm acidity helps balance any oil or butter used in the dish.

Region	Wine
Chinese food	Rieslings and Gewürztraminers pair best with spiced Szechuan or Cantonese food, which can also tolerate a Chenin Blanc if delicately spiced. For heavy northern dishes – such as Peking Duck – try a New World Pinot Noir or Merlot for lush apparent fruit. Rich Shanghai dishes can also benefit from red wine, potentially Californian Zinfandels for a balance between ripe fruit and firm body.
Mexican food	The best advice is to match wines with the predominant sauce or spice in the dish you're about to enjoy. Garlic and onion spiced dishes can do well with a light white (especially if they contain shrimp) whereas chilli dishes might call for Zinfandel or Sangiovese. Try Australian Shiraz with earthy chipotle dishes. A lot of cheese can complicate this, and enchiladas may need an Alsacien Riesling to provide some acid firmness.
Japanese sushi	Delicate fish flavours combined with some rather more robust notes in varied sushi find a natural home alongside sparkling rosé. Delicate red fruit complements rather than overpowers alongside useful acidity and fizz to ensure a clean palate.

Cheeses

Cheese	Wine
Roquefort	Sauternes is an excellent complement to veined blue cheese, with the sweet 'Noble Rot' white complementing the potent salty flavours of the cheese.
Stilton	The classic pairing with port is a valid tradition, again combining sweet lush flavours in the fortified wine with more robust savoury characteristics of the cheese.
Goat's cheese	The particular flavours of these cheeses are perhaps best met with the delightfully tart Loire Sauvignon Blancs, which also contain a grassy note present in the cheese.

(continued)

Cheese	Wine
Cheddar	This can benefit from a bold New World Chardonnay, think a fruit bomb bold Californian or Australian.
Gruyere	Slightly more refined nutty flavours can be balanced well against a Burgundian chardonnay – think Macôn-villages for a balanced accompaniment.
Gorgonzola	Try pairing this buttery blue-vein with the dry, ripe, raisin finish of an Amarone
Brie	This ripe and creamy cheese is best paired with Champagne or other sparkling wine, as the fizz cuts through any flabbiness in the cheese whilst being complemented by white fruit characters.
Mozzarella	Being so fresh and light, mozzarella can be rather dominated by wines. Try a restrained Piedmont Pinot Grigio to complement rather than overpower.
Real stinkers	It's difficult to pair a wine with a truly powerful cheese such as Stinking Bishop, for example, although it can make sense to pair it with a really powerful wine. Try a voluptuous Californian Cabernet or South African Paarl Shiraz.

Vegetarian

When matching wines to vegetarian food follow two simple rules:

1) Strength

The wine should be of a similar strength to your meal. A light, dry white wine will be a good partner for a fresh salad, whilst a full-bodied red will match the strong flavours in a bean cassoulet.

2) Harmony of flavour

Just as when pairing wines with meat dishes, a fundamental rule is that whilst choosing a wine to accompany vegetarian food the flavours match.

There is one more consideration to take into account as a vegetarian or vegan wine-drinker, and that is making sure the wine you are drinking with your meal is as animal-free as the food. As explained in Chapter 1, some fining agents used in wine are animal products, and since there is no comprehensive list of ingredients on a wine bottle which indicate whether or not these are present, your best option is to stick to buying organic or biodynamic wines.

⊣ HOW TO ORDER WINE IN ⊢ A RESTAURANT

Ordering wine in a restaurant can be a daunting experience. However, having read a book such as this and with a calm exploration of the wine list, there is no real pressure from which to shrink. Having the confidence to ask questions is, in turn, the secret to choosing the correct wine.

Although you may be presented with the wine list first, it makes sense to decide on your food before selecting your wine in order to better pair it.

THE WINE LIST

A good wine list should tell you four vital pieces of information about each bottle offered:

1) **The type of wine** – this will indicate which grapes were used so you can get an idea of what flavours to expect.

2) **The producer of the wine** – most helpful if you are looking for a notable winery.

3) **Where it was grown** – as you know, the same grape variety grown in Alsace/Provence/Chile/Australia can produce a very different style of wine, so this is always worth checking.

4) **The vintage** – indicates the year in which the grapes were grown and harvested.

Pocket tip 🍇

Try to avoid wines you've seen in supermarkets or off-licences. Restaurants clearly have a large mark-up, and you're unlikely to be satisfied paying over the odds for a familiar product.

Don't be scared of the 'house wine'. This is inevitably the bottle of which the restaurant sells most and usually represents decent value – a bad 'house wine' does nothing for their reputation. One in four UK diners, however, choose the second cheapest bottle on the wine list – this statistic is no secret and this often represents the highest profit margin bottle on the list. This isn't always true, but be wary of such reflex choices. Often you'll enjoy a wine a lot more by trading up by as little as one or two pounds, as often restaurants operate a 'progressive mark-up' with more expensive bottles actually being closer to their retail price.

That said, don't be afraid to ask questions about any of the bottles or even for some advice on what to order. If your waiter doesn't know what to recommend, there should be a specialist waiter on hand who will.

THE SOMMELIER

This is the specialist wine waiter whose sole responsibility is ensuring that he enables you to choose the right wine for both your dinner and your budget. This is generally the character who both drinks and buys the wine in the restaurant on a full-time basis. Their knowledge and experience is an excellent opportunity for you to ask questions and be guided towards something excellent. Treat them like a friend – there's no need to pretend knowledge nor be ashamed of a lack of it. For best results, be frank about your likes and your budget.

Ask for the sommelier's personal opinions:

- Which list wine do they feel is particularly special?

- Are there any especially good value wines amongst the wine list?

- Do they carry any wines not on the wine list? (Sometimes this question yields some good bin-ends.)

A good sommelier will also ask you about which dishes you have ordered (which meat they are, how they are cooked) and what flavours you enjoy in general to ensure they partner your personal preferences with their perfect grape-based accompaniment.

THE OPENING

When the wine arrives at your table, the waiter will show you the bottle before opening it. Do double check that it is indeed the one you ordered, as busy staff who are rushed off their feet can and do make mistakes so it's always worth a glance.

TASTING THE WINE

This is a slight misnomer as one need only smell the wine at this point. Swirl the glass and smell the wine – any winemaking faults should be immediately obvious by the presence of an acetic or 'off' smell (see p.115 for more on smelling wine). If everything is in order, thank them and withdraw. The waiter will serve any ladies in the party before serving the rest of the table.

> *Remember: this exercise is to check that the wine isn't off and NOT to see if you like it.*

One important point: if the wine turns out to taste corked or of vinegar, the only option is to send it back and the restaurant should not hesitate to offer an alternative.

SERVING THE WINE

Usually at this point a white will be stored in a wine cooler on or next to your table and a red will be left to remain at room temperature. If these attentions are not forthcoming and you are worried that your wine will not stay at its optimum temperature throughout the meal, ask your waiter to provide the props necessary to make it so. In a fine restaurant, the waiter will always pour for diners, although in many more informal restaurants you may happily pour for yourself and others.

Pocket tips on selecting a winner:

- *Argentina, South Africa and the Rhône can often represent better value than either Burgundy or Bordeaux by veering away from name recognition.*
- *New Zealand Sauvignon Blanc presents a standardised style, although prices can be high on this fashionable wine.*
- *Chilean wine in particular can be excellent value – Merlot or Carmenère can be excellent food wines.*
- *Don't be scared of the house wine – it won't change your life but is often good value for money.*
- *Avoid 'second bottle syndrome' and high margin placings – think about your choice and don't make reflex decisions.*
- *If you're eating a difficult-to-pair food (artichoke/asparagus) try some Austrian Grüner Veltliner or Italian Gavi.*
- *Ask your waiter/sommelier! Don't be afraid to ask for opinions.*
- *If you recognise a bottle that you bought off a supermarket shelf, leave it alone. Being aware that the mark-up will most likely make it an unenjoyable bottle!*

⊸ COOKING WITH WINE ⊱

Although some recipes call for a specific type of wine, many merely specify red or white. Don't use your finest bottle but do try a wine before you incorporate it into a dish. The temptation to use poor wine to cook with can spoil a meal, and the price of incorporating a palatable wine is likely to be repaid in flavour.

BUT DOESN'T THE WINE JUST EVAPORATE?

Although a certain amount of the alcohol in a wine will evaporate when you use it in cooking, up to 60% can remain depending on the heat you are cooking at and the amount of booze you added in the first place! Generally, the longer you cook a dish the more alcohol will evaporate away, quite logically.

However, the alcohol content of a dish is the secondary issue to that of flavour. As a wine is heated and cooked, its flavours will concentrate and add their characteristics to your final dish. For example, a fruity wine will endow a dish with an intense fruity quality, whilst a sweet wine will bring out the sweetness in the food (hence why sweet fortified wines such as sherry are often used in desserts).

DEVELOPING YOUR TASTE BUDS

Just as when choosing a wine for a meal you look for qualities similar to that of the food you will be eating, so too do you match these characteristics in your cooking wine. For example:

- If you are cooking a light dish that lays emphasis on herbs, such as chicken with thyme, then add a fruity wine such as Sauvignon Blanc.

- A rich dish in a fruity sauce, such as duck with cherry compote, would benefit from subtle flavour enrichment from a fruity red such as a New World Zinfandel.

- Adding a dash of buttery Chardonnay to your beurre blanc sauce will bring out its creamy qualities whilst adding a touch of bite to this traditional sauce base.

USING WINE OUTSIDE THE POT

Pouring a good dash, or half bottle, of wine into your dish during cooking is just one way of using this versatile ingredient. Why not be daring and use it in some of the following ways.

Marinating

Wine proves a very successful marinade, as the alcohol and acid present in it tenderise the meat before cooking by breaking down its tough fibres. Again, just match your wine to your meat as suggested in the pairing guides.

Deglazing

For those who are as new to cooking as they are to wine, deglazing is the method by which many chefs make the base for their sauces.

After a chef has fried ingredients in a pan and transferred them to another container, the pan will have remnants left in it which will add to the flavour of a sauce. Deglazing is the technique of adding any liquid to this (basically dirty) pan to loosen these bits to incorporate into the subsequent sauce that will be made.

So, in this instance, use wine as your deglazing liquid and the base for the sauce that will accompany your dish. It will be delicious!

Finishing the dish

If you have completed your dish but feel it is a little lacking in some department, adding a soupçon of wine at the end may well be a good option. It is usually only fortified wines that are added at this point as they are already well concentrated so don't really need to be cooked down earlier in the process. Adding a dash of port to an onion gravy or sherry to cream soup will bring it to life in the closing stages.

ᴴ DRINKS TO MAKE USING WINE ᴴ

MULLED WINE

This winter warmer is simple and delicious. You will need:

- 2 bottles red wine (something inexpensive such as a South American Merlot or Carmenere)

- 2 shots of port (preferably an inexpensive brand)

- 3 oranges sliced into sixths with cloves stuck in them (about an inch and a half apart)

- 1 teaspoon of cinnamon

- 1 teaspoon of nutmeg shavings

- Several tablespoons of brown sugar (according to taste)

Put all the ingredients in a large pan and heat gently for about 20 minutes or until hot through. DO NOT ever allow the liquid to boil, as this will burn away the alcohol.

To serve, simply strain out the zest and other gritty bits, and pour into glasses or a festive jug.

RED SANGRIA

This is the perfect thirst quencher for a hot Mediterranean summer afternoon, or even a pleasant English evening in the hazy sunshine. It is also a rather successful wine-based party punch at any time of year!

To make sangria for eight, all you need is:

- 2 bottles of chilled red wine

- 1.5 litres of lemonade or sparkling water (depending on your sweet tooth)

- Selection of different fruits chopped into chunky pieces

- Sugar to taste

- A punch bowl or attractive large serving jug

Quite simply pour in all the ingredients, mix together, serve over ice and enjoy!

CLASSIC CHAMPAGNE COCKTAIL

A slightly more complicated concoction than the simple 'pour into a jug and mix' above, but definitely worth taking your time over to create an elegant aperitif or sumptuous drinks party centrepiece.

To serve eight people you will need:

- 2 bottles of Champagne, which will leave you plenty for those who want another glass

- 8 sugar cubes

- Angostura bitters

- Brandy

There are just four simple steps to creating this cocktail:

1) Pop a sugar cube in the bottom of each glass.

2) Add a dash of Angostura bitters to cover the sugar cube and soak in.

3) Slosh in a nip of brandy (and really, just a nip, although modify to your tastes).

4) Fill to the top with Champagne and enjoy.

BELLINI

This cocktail originated in Italy and remains a very popular cocktail there. Frozen Bellinis are also a popular choice in many bars.

To make Bellini's for four people you will need:

- 2 ripe peaches (or tinned equivalent)

- Chilled sparkling white (traditionally Prosecco)

- Chilled Champagne flutes

Blend the peaches to produce a smoothie-style liquid. Chill this mixture thoroughly in the fridge. Once chilled, fill one-third of a Champagne flute with the peaches and the rest with sparkling white.

BUCKS FIZZ

Bucks Fizz dates back to 1921 when it was invented in the Buck's Club in London. This cocktail can be a favourite breakfast accompaniment.

To make one Bucks Fizz you will need:

- Fresh orange juice

- Champagne

Mix 1 part Champagne (or other affordable sparkling white) with 2 parts chilled orange juice.

KIR ROYAL

This is a French cocktail usually enjoyed as an aperitif.

To make this cocktail you will need:

- Crème de Cassis

- Champagne

Pour the Cassis into the bottom of the glass and top up with Champagne (9 parts Champagne to 1 part Cassis). A Kir cocktail is made exactly the same way using white wine instead of Champagne. A Kir Imperial is also made in the same way using the same measures of raspberry liqueur and Champagne.

6

BUYING WINE

This chapter is intended for both people buying wine for immediate drinking and also those looking for an investment opportunity. The first part of the chapter is intended to guide you through the label of a wine, be able to make informed decisions about which wine you choose.

⤝ UNDERSTANDING THE LABEL ⤞

Labels are perhaps the most confusing aspect of choosing a wine, as they contain a wealth of information that can overwhelm the casual observer. However, by learning to understand the label you will have taken the first step to understanding the process of choosing wines based on your knowledge of regions and grape varieties.

Many New World countries will feature the name of the grape on the label. This is the simplest method for any wine drinker to shop for favoured varieties. Australian, American, South American and Kiwi producers all tend to list a single grape variety or the principal grapes in the blend of their wines. Grape variety and vintage will often be the most prominent, followed by the name of the producer and the area the wine comes from. In general, the better a wine the more specific the label will be about where it came from. A wine marked only 'Australian' will likely be a standardised blend from across many regions whilst, for example a wine labelled 'Barossa Valley' is more likely to be the output of an individual winery.

This is a perfectly acceptable and enjoyable way to tour the wines of the world. However, this becomes problematic when faced with French labels, which seldom list grape varieties and rely on consumer knowledge.

READING A WINE LABEL

This mock-up of a generic label is designed to give an example of how an *Appellation d'Origine Controlée* (AC or AOC) classified French wine might be labelled:

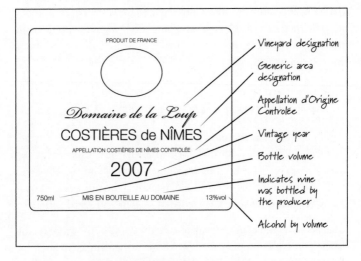

- The **Vineyard Designation** is not a strictly regulated piece of information – this may just as well be the name of the wine given to it by the producer.

- The **Generic Area Designation** is a recognisable place that is often the same as the AC.

- The **Appellation d'Origine Controlée (AOC)** is the most important piece of information on the label – it tells you that the wine was made in a certain area, using certain permitted grape varieties, within certain strict guidelines bound by law. These factors change from area to area, although some insight into these varied practices is given in Chapter 3 (p.22).

● The **Vintage Year** is an important declaration, as if a year is declared then the majority of the grapes used must come from within that year.

● The **Bottle Volume** and **Alcohol by Volume (ABV)** are standard, self-explanatory, regulatory inclusions.

● Some producers include the phrase *'Mis en bouteille au Domaine'* – this merely indicates that the producer has bottled the wine and has not sold their grapes to a cooperative or merchant. You might also look out for the phrase with 'Château' instead of Domaine. Watching out for these phrases can be an excellent way to choose hand-crafted individual wines with a sense of identity.

APPELLATIONS

Appellation systems are complicated and diverse, yet they are also excellent guarantors of quality. These designations are governed by law, and producers who transgress can be tried for fraud.

Appellations of Origin can govern all or some of the following.

● Geographic limits of the production area, often limited by soil.

● The density of planting within vineyards.

● The pruning style of the viticulturist and standards to be upheld.

● The yields of grapes per hectare of vineyard.

● Wines may be subjected to a tasting by a certification panel.

● Permitted grape varieties will be outlined.

● Trellis and training systems may be dictated (ie how the vines are grown).

● Winemaking techniques, including maturation and compulsory aging.

● Lab analysis of standards of clarity, alcohol level, etc.

In Italy, Spain and Germany similar guidelines apply as in France. The label will list appellations and producers, but seldom grape varieties. Some Spanish wines such as Rioja will also carry an extra age statement (Crianza, Reserva, etc) – these are listed in Chapter 3 (p.105).

European appellation systems are tiered in descending order of quality within each nation.

France

Appellation d'Origine Controlée (AC or AOC):	The highest classification that a French wine can normally attain with strict regional guidelines which are actively enforced. Within each wine region there are geographic hierarchies of AC – the more specific of which demand higher standards and enforce stricter regulations.
Vins Délimités de Qualité Supérieure (VDQS):	This was originally designed as a stepping stone to AC classification but has declined in popularity. Represents wines that have been strictly enforced produced in a specific area and subject to panel tasting.
Vins de Pays	These are generally locally produced wines that distinguish themselves in some way from *Vins de Table* and are limited by some regulations such as yields and grape variety.
Vins de Table	Basic table wine production.

Italy

Denominazione di Origine Controllata e Garantita (DOCG)	The highest quality wines, denoting a very specific and narrow region, operating according to very strict guidelines. Must carry a seal on the neck to demonstrate it is genuine.

Denominazione di Origine Controllata (DOC)	Defines a specific area using specific methods. Quality wines.
Indicazione Geographica Typica (IGT)	Defines wide regions and is the newest classification type – can hide some excellent surprises (e.g. Super-Tuscans).
Vina de Tavola	The most basic category of table wine.

Spain

Denominación de Pago (DO de Pago)	Individual single-estates with an international reputation – there are only seven of these.
Denominación de Origen Calificada (DOCa)	Top-quality wine regions including Rioja and Priorat.
Denominación de Origen (DO)	Mainstream quality -wine regions outside of the paramount classifications.
Vino de Calidad Producido en Región Determinada (VCPRD)	Less strict regulations with a specific geographical point of origin.
Vino de Mesa	Basic table wine production.

Portugal

Denominação de Origem Controlada (DOC)	Wines of a controlled geographical origin, according to strict production rules.
Indicação de Proveniência Regulamentada (IPR)	Designates wines of a specific origin with less strict rules than the DOC areas.
Vinho Regional	Table wines made in a specific region.
Vinho de Mesa	Basic table wines produced in Portugal.

Germany

Qualitätswein mit Prädikat (QmP)	The highest appellation which regulates wine origin, varietals and producer.
Qualitätswein bestimmter Anbaugebiete (QbA)	Quality wines from specific areas and subject to regulation.
Landwein	Basic table wine with some indication of origin.
Deutscher Tafelwein	Table wine without any indication of origin, possibly mixed with other European wines.

(Subdivisions of German appellations are dealt with on p.73)

In all these countries the production of **table wine** is a classification for wines which do not qualify for any higher berth in the
prevailing appellation system. This can be because of quality but
also because of methods – many innovative French producers put
out table wine as they are trying new methods and new grape varieties within areas of fixed tradition. You can find exceptional
value alongside very basic wine – this is a category better worth
exploring whilst visiting the area as local knowledge trumps any
guide book.

*'It is well to remember that there are five reasons for drinking: the
arrival of a friend; one's present or future thirst; the excellence of the
wine; or any other reason.'*
Latin saying

⊷ WHERE TO BUY WINE? ⊷

It is easy to buy excellent wine these days. The wine industry
worldwide has improved sufficiently in the last 20 years so that
there is very little poor wine on sale. The key is to know what you
are buying, and to make sure you get what you want. Hopefully
this book will help you with that.

Pocket tip 🍇

*Some stores offer good wine advice in store, which is often
worth taking. Try to assess whether the person giving the advice
really knows what they are talking about or not, and whether
they have listened properly to any questions you have put to
them.*

SUPERMARKETS

Supermarkets now account for a large proportion of all wine
bought. This gives their buyers excellent buying power, and as a

result you can often get outstanding wine at reasonable prices. Some supermarket chains consistently offer great quality wines, Marks & Spencer and Waitrose in particular, but all the leading chains have good selections.

WINE MERCHANTS

Whether chain stores or independent, wine merchants can also offer good ranges and excellent advice – but not all do, so be careful. It is well worth trying a few until you find one which gives you the range and advice you want. The rise in wine purchases at supermarkets has put many high street 'off-licences' out of business. Those that remain often have specialisms, for example Nicolas is a chain with a very wide range of French wine but relatively little from elsewhere. Berry Brothers & Rudd and Lay & Wheeler are two small groups of high-quality wine merchants well worth considering. If you want some of the smaller producers' top-quality wines from the New World, in particular, you will almost certainly need to find a wine merchant.

SMALLER CHAINS AND INDEPENDENT STORES

These may lack the major buying power of say a supermarket, but they are able to buy from smaller producers who could not offer the volume a supermarket would need, and therefore often have a different range of wines.

WINE CLUB

Many people buy wine from a wine club, by far the largest of these being *The Sunday Times* Wine Club (www.sundaytimeswineclub.co.uk; 0845 217 9122). This tends to involve a mixed case of wine being sent to you every month, and can be a wonderful way to try a variety of wines. The key is to keep notes about what you like so you can buy more if you want to.

ONLINE

There are some brilliant opportunities to buy excellent wine online, especially fine wine which can be stored properly and listed online rather than displayed in direct sunlight in a shop window. Ensure that you use a reputable retailer, however. Try: www.wine-searcher.com – www.winestore.co.uk – www.every-wine.co.uk. The internet can also be an excellent place to buy wine accessories from companies such as Cork & Foil.

The Wine Society

The Wine Society consistently wins 'wine retailer of the year' awards and is special enough to deserve a brief mention here. It is a not-for-profit company, owned by and created for the benefit of its members. You need to be a member to be able to buy from it, but joining is relatively simple; you don't need to know people or have gone to a certain school to be able to join! The society offers a wide range of excellent wines via a catalogue and its website. It sells plenty of good, inexpensive wines as well as some of the world's very best wines, and is well worth considering.
www.thewinesociety.com; 01438 737700

⊸ INVESTING IN WINE ⊶

'Good wine ruins the purse; bad wine ruins the stomach'
Spanish saying

Stocks and shares are notoriously fickle investment opportunities; there is the possibility of making millions, or of losing your investment. As people increasingly get burned on the stock market, attention is growing around a potentially lucrative investment opportunity: wine.

If you can get the price and the timing of your investment right, the rewards can be great. A bottle of 1886 Château Lafite-Rothschild Bordeaux, bought in 2005 for £3,150, would now be worth £9,600 — that's a 200% return!

> *'I like best the wine drunk at the cost of others.'*
> Diogenes the Cynic

Of course, this is an extreme example and investing in wine is by no means a 'safe' option for your cash. Nonetheless, there is evidence that historically fine wines have proved to be a solid long-term investment opportunity, averaging returns of around 12% a year.

WHERE DO YOU START?

- The most fundamental aspect of successful wine investment is finding yourself a reputable, long-established wine merchant who will advise you on what and when to purchase, whilst potentially telling you when to sell. A good cautionary website to consult to get yourself well informed on the topic is www.investdrinks.org.

- Be aware that, to invest in wine, you need two things: money and patience. In the first five years of investment you can expect to spend between £5,000 and £10,000 as a modest estimate. As you are not advised to sell for five to 10 years, it will be a while before you can reap the rewards of your investment.

Pocket tip 🍇

Many merchants run 'bin clubs' where investors can contribute £100 a month and wines are bought on their behalf throughout the year. If you don't have £5,000 to spare, this could prove a cheaper way to get your foot on the investment ladder and start learning the ins and outs of the wine market.

WHICH WINES SHOULD YOU INVEST IN?

Choosing wines to invest in can be a bit of a minefield. But this needn't be the case if you look for at least four of the following five indicators in your investment wine:

1) Choose an instantly recognisable label or brand with a good record of quality and fetching high prices.

2) Your wine must come from a good vintage and be highly rated by wine critics around the world.

3) It should have the ability to age and improve over time, so the longer you keep hold of it, the greater your profits will become.

4) Check to see if previous vintages of the wine you are thinking of investing in have retained consistent demand as this is a good indicator of whether it will be popular on the market.

5) Any wine you invest in should have a history of a consistent upward price movement.

Most money is made buying Bordeaux *en primeur*. This means that you reserve the wine before it is bottled, which usually happens after an exceptionally good vintage such as that of 2008. This market has soared and getting in can be a bit of a scrum but ultimately very valuable.

Prestige Australian wines are also developing in price, and some investors are looking to this relatively under-valued market as a means of avoiding the crowds. Bottles of Penfold's Grange retail for several hundred pounds unaged.

Investing in wine dos and don'ts

Do find a reputable wine merchant or investment company that you can trust and listen to their advice.

Do develop a good relationship with your specialist merchant as you will get better advice and first offer of the more highly sought after wines.

Do store your wine in perfect conditions so it will mature predictably. The best option is to keep it in bond with a specialist wine storage company or merchant.

Do buy wine that you can drink if it all goes down the drain – remember, you can't drink stock options.

Don't expect instant high returns. Wine values tend to increase over long periods of time, so investing in a good Bordeaux tomorrow won't mean it is ready to sell in one year's time and you can retire on the proceeds!

Don't buy investment wine on a whim, stick to the tried and tested investment wines that perform well year on year.

The most prestigious of the names mentioned in Chapter 3 are the best names to invest in, as brands mean everything when it comes to century old Châteaux.

7

STORING WINE

There are important factors to consider about both the environment in which you will store your wine and also about the wine itself which you are intending to age.

Choosing a place to store your wine is important if you are serious about aging wine. It can also be important if you simply want to ensure that a bottle you're keeping for a special occasion is in prime condition for that moment.

Places such as a cupboard, a garage, a disused fireplace, a pantry or a basement are all good locations for storing wine. Although these may seem like fairly odd choices, they rely on a simple harmony of factors which allows for the successful cellaring of wine. There are also wine shops which offer cellaring as well as specific professional cellaring companies and bonded warehouses. These services may be necessary for the wine investor buying cases of *en primeur* Bordeaux, yet it is just as possible to store fine wine in your own home, as long as the environment is right.

You may have been told to store wine in a cool, dark place – this is partially correct, but requires qualification.

⊶ WAYS OF STORING WINE ⊷

TEMPERATURE CONTROLLED WINE CABINET

These look somewhat like a refrigerator in appearance but keep your wine at a constant optimal temperature. These are perfect storage devices but be mindful of capacity if you imagine your collection growing. Eurocave make an excellent range of wine cabinets which are designed specifically to house your wine in pristine conditions.

TEMPERATURE AND HUMIDITY CONTROL MACHINES

The most basic piece of equipment you could hope for is a thermometer which measures the highest and lowest temperatures of any particular day. These will inform you if you need to take any measures to alter an unacceptable variable temperature range. You can buy conditioning units which ensure that the optimal temperature and humidity are maintained, operating much like a conventional air conditioner but with more focus on humidity. If you are using such conditioning equipment, it may be worth purchasing an insulated door, to ensure the complete effectiveness of temperature and humidity control. These are available widely from companies such as Autour du Vin.

HOLE-IN-THE-GROUND CELLARS

It is possible to contact companies and have them construct a custom cellar for those with only a little space that lack a decent storage place for their wine. Spiral cellars is a company that will dig a hole to house a spiral staircase with walls which are lined with wine racks. Good insulation ensures that temperature variation is not a problem whilst passive ventilation ensures humidity is kept optimal.

⌁ ENVIRONMENTAL FACTORS ⌁

TEMPERATURE

Cool temperatures help age wine properly, encouraging the development of natural chemical reactions within the bottle that lend aged wines their specific characteristics. Ideally there should not be wide swings in temperature as this will damage wine. Exceptionally cool temperatures will retard aging (below 5°C) whilst excessive heat (above 20°C) will accelerate aging unadvisedly. The table gives recommended temperatures for storing different types of wine:

Type of wine	Ideal storage temperature °C
Red Wine	12–14
Dry whites and rosé	8–14
Sparkling wines and Champagne	6–8

HUMIDITY

Wine is best stored in cellars that are not too dry, as this will encourage adverse ullage. The term 'ullage' describes the space between cork and wine which can develop in very old bottles, increasing the likelihood that a cork will allow the passage of wine into the bottle. Excess humidity can cause mould and ruin labels.

LIGHT

Excessive light in the cellar will almost certainly interfere with the temperature and adversely affect the wine. The colour of the bottle glass will also determine the vulnerability of the wine to light, with clear glass bottles being the most at risk. Sparkling wines respond worst to excess light. This is the principal reason that most wine storage areas are in basements or cellars, as light is unlikely to cause too much of a problem.

VIBRATION

Aging wine is meant to be left to rest undisturbed by movement and noise – unfortunate if you live beneath a train line. Excess vibration will not allow the wine to gather proper sediment and will unsettle the aging process accordingly. Watch out for washing machines, generators or refrigerator motors causing excess vibrations.

STORAGE ANGLE

Making sure that wines are stored label up is an important if obvious point. It prevents excess movement of the bottle in identifying the wine and also allows for the proper development of sediment on the translucent underbelly of the bottle. It also prevents damage to the label, which it is important to keep in good condition if you intend to sell the bottle at a later date. It is possible to buy protective covers for labels from wineries and online retailers.

Horizontal storage also ensures that the wine remains in contact with the cork, preventing the penetration of oxygen and resultant oxidisation. This horizontal storage is a consistent rule for all wines and port. Fortified wines (except for port) should always be stored upright however.

VENTILATION

Proper ventilation will not only help ensure better humidity in most areas but also that lingering odours in the cellar do not adversely affect corks and therefore your wine.

⊸ CHOOSING WINES TO AGE ⊱

It can be difficult to choose exactly which wines one wants to age, particularly with the predominance of supermarket retailers and brand name wines. Not all wines benefit from aging. Some are made to be drunk young and others will only taste past their best if left for a year or more in the cellar.

A decent operating principle is that wines of under £15 are unlikely to require aging. A more specific principle is to ask the person from whom you are buying the wine as they will likely be happy to advise you.

Below are examples of some wines which it might be prudent to consider cellaring, although clearly it is only a sample and not comprehensive.

Red wines

- Quality Bordeaux Châteaux

- Grand or Premier Cru Burgundy

- Barolo, Chianti, Brunell di Montalcino and other quality Italian reds

- Rioja and Ribera del Duero

- Quality Californian Cabernet Sauvignons

- Hermitage, Châteauneuf-du-Pape and Côte Rotie from the Rhône

- Quality Shiraz from Australia

White wines

- Fine German Rieslings

- Burgundian Chardonnays

- Alsacien Riesling and Gewürztraminer

Sparkling wines

- Vintage Champagnes and Prestige Cuvées

Other wines

- Sauternes

- Tokaji Aszu

- Fortified wines such as Madeira and Port

⊶ CELLAR TIPS ⊷

ORGANISATION

It might seem an obvious point, but organisation can prevent frustration in searching for a wine and also damage caused by shifting bottles unnecessarily.

Consider organising your wines by region, vintage or some other personal system. Do, however, make a note of this system. It is well worth keeping a notebook or some other record of what wines you have – this will prevent accidental over-aging or confusion about how long something has been in the cellar. Databases work well if you're technically minded and allow you to search a particularly large collection.

ACCESSIBILITY

Although some independent wine merchants kindly offer a cellaring service, this can be a problem if they operate irregular or short hours. It is important to remember that at the moment you may want to open a long-saved bottle for a visiting friend that store may be closed.

⊶ LEVEL OF WINE ⊷

When aging wine for a long period (10 years or over) one can expect the level of the wine in the bottle to fall. It is important, however, to ensure that the level does not fall too drastically as this can indicate a problem with the cellaring.

Describing the level of wine can be important when it comes to the sale of wine, and fine wine will often be sold with a reference to its fill level. Here is a summary of the terms used.

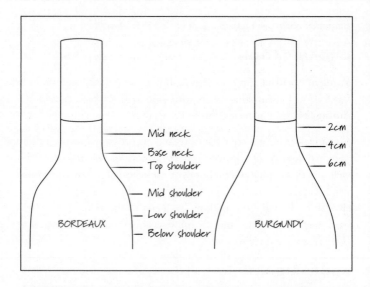

Bordeaux bottles

Mid Neck	Indicates good storage and very little or no aging. If an extremely old wine has this level it can indicate reconditioning. Reconditioning was the practice of a producer professionally rebottling old wine, which has thankfully now fallen into almost total disuse as it was recognised as a licence for fraud.
Base Neck	A standard fill level in a modern wine. An aged bottle (over 10 years) with this level has been superbly stored for its lifetime.
Top Shoulder	Acceptable in wines of around 10 years. Older wines filled to Top Shoulder have no doubt seen excellent cellaring.
Mid Shoulder	Not unusual for wines of 50 years and over. This is a risky condition in which to buy wine as it could indicate poor storage.
Low Shoulder	Indicates that the wine has very probably been held in poor storage conditions and may well be undrinkable.
Below Shoulder	This is an unusually low level, indicating that the wine is almost certainly undrinkable – would only be sold in the case of a particularly rare label or bottle.

Burgundy bottles

Around 2cm	An exemplary fill level for any age of wine.
Around 3cm	Normal for wines up to 12 years. Exceptional for older wines.
Around 4cm	Normal for wines of around 20 years, exceptional for older and worrying for younger.
Around 5cm	Although this level is possible in wines of older than 30 years, it may indicate some damage to the wine.
Around 6cm	Almost definitely undrinkable although may be offered for sale if the bottle or label is exceptionally prized.

8

WINE AND HEALTH

'Drink no longer water, but use a little wine for thy stomach's sake and thine often infirmities'
1 Timothy, 5:23

Wine in moderation can provide an excellent supplement to one's health and well-being. This section aims to highlight some of the real benefits that enjoying a glass or two of wine can provide before moving on to explain the exact details of what moderation involves.

~~~| BENEFITS |~~~

The medical profession has recognised the health benefits of wine for thousands of years, and Hippocrates himself recommended its use for various ailments way back in 450BC. Although it is only in recent years that we have begun to be able to scientifically prove that wine can be beneficial for health, its antiseptic, antibacterial and cathartic qualities have long been enjoyed by our ancestors across the globe.

Particularly interesting is the 'French Paradox', which has puzzled scientists over the last few decades. Dieticians were at a loss to explain how it was that in the regions of France which had some of the highest levels of saturated fat in food, residents displayed low levels of heart disease and cholesterol. Many now believe that the moderate consumption of red wine throughout their adult life has helped improve the health of these regions, and that this is a transferable benefit.

A HEALTHY HEART

Moderate wine consumption has been shown in medical studies to correlate with a lower incidence of coronary heart disease. Wine contains compounds known as flavanoids that may give protection from cellular damage and cancer formation, and which are also responsible for promoting a more healthy cardiovascular system.

One form of flavanoid, oligomeric procyanidin, has recently been proven to prevent hardening of the arteries, whilst resveratrol and quercetin have shown the potential to protect against heart disease. Another recent study indicated that resveratrol can inhibit the formation of the protein that causes cardio fibrosis, which inhibits healthy heart function during times of stress.

It is also common knowledge that red wine in moderation can help to balance cholesterol. Some medical professionals ascribe this benefit to the fact that wine slows down digestion, preventing some of the fatty content of meals entering into the bloodstream. Neither enjoying a meal at length nor lingering over a glass of wine present arduous chores, so why not do it for your doctor.

Recent scientific studies have shown that red wine in particular can help the digestion of certain foods including red meat, as it breaks down and removes potentially harmful compounds called lipid hydroperoxides and malonaldehydes. This also helps to prevent peptic ulcers.

WINE AND CANCER PREVENTION

Wine has been shown in some situations to reduce the occurrence of certain cancers, such as those of the digestive tract. The flavanoids and other compounds found in wine are believed to function as anti-oxidants and prevent molecules known as free-radicals from causing cellular damage that can lead to cancer.

Two other compounds found in grape skins, resveratrol and quercetin, have been shown through laboratory studies to help boost the immune system and block cancer formation.

Pocket fact 🍷

A consultant cardiologist called Dr William McCrea once prescribed two glasses of red wine a day to his heart patients in a Swindon hospital, after studies showed that if people who have had a heart attack drink moderate amounts of red wine, this reduces their chance of getting a second heart attack by 50%. The wine in question was a Chilean Cabernet Sauvignon. It is doubtful whether your GP will issue you a prescription for a case of red wine, but you can always ask!

ANTI-AGING

Resveratrol, the miracle compound found in wine, is claimed to have the ability to activate a class of longevity genes in the body known as sirtuins which reduce cellular decay. In doing this, it gives cells more opportunity to re-grow and repair, which can slow down aging processes both inside and out.

Preliminary European studies of resveratrol have also suggested that it can significantly reduce the development of neurodegenerative diseases such as Alzheimer's and Parkinson's.

'If God forbade drinking, would He have made wine so good?'
Cardinal Richeleu

WINE AND WOMEN

Moderate consumption of wine has been shown to reduce the risk of women developing kidney stones by up to 59%.

Post-menopausal women also benefit from drinking wine, with a lower level of diabetes strongly linked. Wine drinkers have lower insulin levels and respond better to the introduction of insulin into the blood, putting them less at risk from type 2 diabetes.

⊶| EVERYTHING IN MODERATION |⊶

The health benefits found in people who drink wine were limited to those who drank regularly but in moderation. Over-indulgence is universally regarded as far more harmful than total abstinence.

SO HOW MUCH IS MODERATE?

The government guidelines recommend not exceeding the following daily intake:

- Women: No more than 2/3 units a day
- Men: No more than 3/4 units each day

It is also advised to have at least two alcohol-free days each week alongside these limits.

WHAT MAKES UP A UNIT?

The simple answer to this is, surprisingly little:

- Half a small glass (175ml) of wine
- 25ml sherry, vermouth or liqueur
- Half a pint of standard strength (3.5% ABV) beer, cider or lager
- 25ml of spirit

Smaller wine glasses of 125ml used to be the norm in bars and pubs, although this has crept up to 175ml in recent years. Draft Government proposals could see the compulsory offering of smaller glasses alongside existing sizes to allow for greater choice.

To calculate the number of alcohol units in a drink, the sum is simple:

$$\text{Strength (ABV)} \times \text{volume (ml)} \div 1{,}000 = \text{No. of units}$$

Using this equation we can work out the units of any volume of wine. For example, a standard 75cl bottle at a fairly average 13% ABV would be 9.75 units, a higher 15% ABV would be 11.25 units and so on.

⊶ WATCHING YOUR WAISTLINE ⊷

Despite certain health benefits associated with wine, alcohol in general provides empty calories from a nutritional point of view. If you want to indulge without ruining your figure, however, here is a guideline to the calorie content of popular beverages per standard pub serving:

Wine	Calories
175ml wine, dry white	116
175ml wine, medium white	130
175ml wine, red	119
175ml wine, rosé	124
175ml wine, sparkling	130
175ml Champagne	133
50ml port	78

⊷ WHEN NOT TO DRINK WINE ⊶

Although generally when drunk in moderation, wine can be enjoyed by most adults, there are occasions when it is best avoided. The UK Government and the NHS recommend that you should not drink alcohol given the following circumstances:

- Pre-menopausal women with a family history of breast cancer should not drink any alcohol at all.

- When taking certain over-the-counter or prescription drugs (consult a doctor or pharmacist).

- If you have inflammation of the digestive tract, peptic ulcers, liver disease, pancreatitis, kidney or urinary infections, prostate disorders or epilepsy.

- If you are in the 1% of the population who are allergic to sulphites. Reactions include restricted breathing ability, skin rashes, hives and nausea.

'What though youth gave love and roses age still leaves us friends and wine.'
Thomas Moore

GLOSSARY

Abboccato	Italian, meaning 'slightly sweet'.
ABV	Alcohol by volume; the percentage of alcohol in the wine.
Adega	Portuguese, meaning cellar.
Ah-So	A wine opener with two parallel prongs that gently rock a cork out of a bottle, also known as the butler's friend.
Amabile	Italian, meaning 'semi-sweet'.
Anbaugebiete	Any of the 13 wine regions recognised under German wine law *Qualitätswein bestimmter Anbaugebiete*.
Annatta	Italian, meaning 'vintage'.
Apéritif/Aperitivo	French/Italian, meaning something alcoholic that is drunk before a meal to stimulate the appetite.
Appellation	A protected name under which wine is sold. It indicates the specific region grapes have been grown in, such as California or Burgundy.
Appellation d'Origine Contrôlée (AOC)	The French quality control system for wine, see p.152.
Aroma	The fragrant quality of a wine.
Ausbruch	Austrian wine that is very sweet, having been affected by *Botrytis cinerea*, see p.7.
Barrique	The standard wine storage barrel of Bordeaux; capacity 225 litres.
Beerenauslese	German or Austrian wines that are extremely sweet having been affected by *Botrytis cinerea*.
Bentonite	An aluminium silicate clay formed from volcanic ash that is used to clarify wine.
Blanc/Bianco/Branco	French/Italian/Portuguese, meaning 'white'.

Blanc de Blancs	French, meaning white wine (usually sparkling) made from white grapes.
Blanc de Noirs	French, meaning white wine (usually sparkling) made using red grapes.
Blush wine	See Rosé.
Bodega	Spanish, meaning 'winery' or 'wine cellar'.
Botrytis cinerea	Also known commonly as 'Noble Rot'; a fungus that affects grapes, causing them to produce intensely sweet wines, see p.7.
Bouquet	Similar to 'aroma' but used on more mature wines that will have more complex smells.
Brut	Means 'very dry' and is used to describe Champagne and sparkling wines.
Bung	The plug/hole in a wine barrel through which it can be filled and emptied.
Cantina	Italian, meaning 'wine cellar'.
Cantina Sociale	Italian, meaning 'cooperative winery'.
Carbonic Maceration	A grape crushing process by which grapes are piled on top of one another in a vat, so those at the bottom become pressed into juice.
Cava	Spanish sparkling wine.
Cave	French, meaning 'cave' and used to denote an underground wine storage facility. Often indicates a cooperative venture.
Chai	French, meaning a cellar in which wine is stored and aged.
Chapitalisation	Adding sugar to wine before or during the fermentation process to increase the final alcohol level. Named after Dr Chaptal, who developed the process.
Château	Referring to a French grand estate, equivalent to a stately home, often denoting a long-established and successful winery.
Claret	Originates from the French 'clairet', meaning light red wine and used to describe the dry red wine from Bordeaux.
Colheita	Portuguese, meaning 'vintage'.
Consorzio	An Italian winegrowers' association.
Corkage	In a restaurant where you can bring your own wine, this is the fee they charge to open it for you.
Cosecha	Spanish, meaning 'vintage'.

Coulure	The non-pollination of vine blossoms, usually caused by bad weather.
Crémant	French, denoting a moderately sparkling wine that is not as fizzy as Champagne.
Cru	French, meaning 'growth'; refers to the quality of the vineyard.
Cuvée	French, meaning the blend of grapes; most often used in terms of making Champagne.
Decant	Pouring wine from the bottle into a different container to remove the sediment and allow the wine to breathe.
Dégorgement	Freezing and removing the end of a bottle of sparkling wine to extract residual yeast, see p.9.
Demi-sec	French, meaning 'half-dry' but actually meaning sweet when describing Champagne.
Denominação de Origem Controlada (DO)	The Portuguese quality control system that guarantees the quality of wine and its origins.
Denominación de Origen/ Denominación de Origen Calificada (DOC)	The two Spanish quality control systems that guarantee the quality of wine and its origins. The latter denotes far higher quality wines than the former.
Denominazione di Origine Controllata e Garantita (DOCG)	The Italian quality control system that guarantees the quality of wine and its origins.
Destemming	The process by which grape stems are removed prior to fermentation to limit the amount of tannins in the final wine.
Dolce/Doce/Doux/ Dulce	Italian/Portuguese/French/Spanish, meaning 'sweet'.
Domaine	French, meaning 'wine estate'.
Dosage	A sweetening liqueur added to Champagne to create the final flavour.
Effervescence	The bubbles of gas in a sparkling wine/Champagne.
Eiswein	German, meaning 'Ice Wine'. Denotes wines that are made from grapes that have been left on the vines to freeze during winter, and which subsequently produce extremely sweet wines, see p.7.
En primeur	The process of buying wine before it has been bottled and released on the market, most

	commonly practised by wine investors as wines generally go up in price once they are bottled.
En tirage	The time that Champagne and sparkling wines are left in the bottle to age, both during the secondary fermentation process and afterwards.
Espumante/Espumoso	Portuguese/Spanish, meaning 'sparkling'.
Fermentation	The conversion of sugar in grape juice to alcohol and carbon dioxide through a reaction with yeast.
Fiasco	Italian, denotes the straw-encased bottles that are used for fairly low-quality Chianti.
Fining	Process in winemaking by which undesirable particles that can cloud wine or alter its taste are removed.
Frizzante	Italian, meaning 'fizzy'. Can be used to refer to a sparkling wine, or when wine causes a tingling sensation on the tongue.
Gallo Nero	The black rooster used on the labels of Chianti DOCG.
Garrafeira	Portuguese, denoting a high-quality wine.
Grand Cru	French, meaning 'great growth'. Used to indicate that wine has come from the very best vineyards in Burgundy.
Grand Cru Classé	French, meaning 'great classed growth' and used to denote wine from the second highest quality level of vineyards that are found in St-Émilion in Bordeaux.
Hectare	Measure of vineyard area. Equivalent to 10,000 square metres or 2.471 acres.
Horizontal tasting	When different wines from the same vintage are tasted in comparison to one another.
Institut Nationale des Appellations d'Origine	The French wine governing body that manages the AOC system.
Joven	Spanish, refers to a young wine (sold under one year of harvest) that has had little or no oak aging.
Kabinett	Dry, light wines from Germany and Austria.
Late Harvest	A style of sweet wine made from grapes that are very ripe having been harvested later in the year.
Lees	The deposit of yeast and other by-products left in the bottom of a fermentation tank.
Legs	The droplets that form and run down the sides of a wine glass after the wine has been swirled, indicating the alcoholic content of the wine.

Length	The amount of time that the aromas of a wine linger in the mouth after it has been swallowed.
Maceration	The length of time for which the grape skins stay in contact with the juice during fermentation.
Madeira	A fortified wine from Madeira Island, just off the coast of Portugal.
Maderize	A term used to describe an oxidised wine, which will develop a sweet flavour and a brownish tint.
Maduro	Portuguese, meaning 'mature'.
Malolactic Fermentation	An optional fermentation process in which bacteria converts malic acid into lactic acid and carbon dioxide, which results in a softer tasting, smoother drinking wine.
Méthode Champenoise	The traditional method of making Champagne or sparkling wine in which secondary fermentation takes place inside the bottle, see p.9.
Millésime	French, meaning 'vintage'.
Muselet	The wire cage that holds a Champagne cork in the bottle.
Must	Grape juice prior to, or during, fermentation.
New World wines	Wines produced in countries that are either fairly new to winemaking or which lie outside the established European vineyards. These include Chile, Australia, South Africa, New Zealand and the USA.
Noble Rot	See *Botrytis cinerea*.
Non-vintage	A wine that is made without a majority of its grapes coming from the same year.
Nose	See *Aroma*.
Oak	The most commonly used wood in the aging process; imparts new flavour dimensions and increases tannins in wine.
Oeil de Perdrix	French, meaning 'partridge eye'. Used to describe the colour of a pale rosé.
Oenology	The science of making wine (encompasses *Viticulture* and *Viniculture*).
Old World wines	Wines from long-established wine-growing regions in Europe, including France, Germany, Italy, Spain and Portugal.

Organic	Organic grapes are grown without the use of chemicals such as pesticides or fertilisers. Organic wines are produced without the addition of extra sulphites during fermentation and bottling.
Oxidation	Occurs in wine that has been over-exposed to air. Usually results in the wine taking on a stale aroma and a brownish tint.
Pétillant	Denotes a French wine that is slightly sparkling.
Petrol Nose	A distinctive characteristic found in older varieties of Riesling that is actually highly prized, as it is more agreeable than it first sounds!
Phenolic Compounds	The tannins, pigments and flavanoids found in grape skins.
Pigeage	The traditional act of stomping grapes underfoot in open fermentation tanks.
Port	Fortified wine from the Oporto region of Portugal.
Premier Cru	French, meaning 'first growth'. Indicates the highest quality French wines produced in the best vineyards.
Premier Grand Cru Classé	French, meaning 'first great classed growth'. Used only to denote the highest quality wines from St-Émilion.
Punt	The conical hollow in the bottom of wine bottles that supposedly reinforces the bottle and catches the sediment.
Racking	The process in winemaking by which the clear liquid that rises to the top of the fermentation vat is siphoned off and away from the dregs of fruit skin, yeast and other particles that have collected at the bottom of the tank.
Reserva	A Spanish wine matured for at least three years (red) or two years (white) and with one year spent maturing in oak barrels.
Reserve	A term used by wineries to denote a grape selection that is highly specialised and should therefore produce a high-quality wine.
Residual sugar	The amount of leftover sugar in a wine after fermentation.
Rojo/Rosso	Spanish/Italian, meaning 'red'.
Rosado/Rosato	Portuguese and Spanish/Italian, meaning 'rosé'.
Rosé	Common term for pink or rose-coloured wine.
Seco/Séco	Spanish/Portuguese, meaning 'dry'.

Sediment	Particles that settle at the bottom of a wine, most commonly older red wines.
Sekt	German, denoting a quality sparkling wine.
Sommelier	A specialist wine waiter found in top restaurants who can help advise on choosing wine to go with a meal.
Sulphite	Occurs as a natural by-product of fermentation. Additional quantities are sometimes added to wine in order to preserve it for longer lengths of time once bottled, see p.11.
Super Tuscans	An unofficial category of high-quality Tuscan wines, including Piedmont and Veneto. The phrase refers to a wine made outside of traditional appellation rules, but within the region of Tuscany.
Table wine	Any wine that is not sparkling or fortified, so just red, white or rosé varieties not qualifying for higher regional appellations.
Tannins	Naturally occurring compounds in plants that create a defence mechanism through leaving a bitter, astringent taste in the mouth which dissuades animals from eating them. In winemaking, they are found in grape skins and help to impart flavour and colour to wines (red in particular).
Terroir	The golden phrase of French winemaking which encapsulates the entire situation of the vine (soil, climate and grape variety). Terroir is regarded with almost religious fervour as a viticultural 'holy trinity' that defines the produce of a vineyard and a region.
Trichloroanisole (TCA)	This chemical is responsible for wine becoming corked. It is found in 3%–5% of all wines made, and is usually a result of corks that haven't been cleaned properly after bleaching. It causes wine to take on a mouldy aroma of old socks and to taste even worse.
Trockenbeerenauslese	Very sweet German and Austrian wines that have been made using grapes affected by Botrytis cinerea.
Vendemmia/Vendimia	Italian/Spanish, meaning 'vintage'.
Verde	Portuguese, meaning 'young'.
Vertical tasting	When different vintages of the same wine are tasted.

Vielles vignes	French, meaning 'old vines'. Denotes vines that are well established and renowned for producing low-volume yields.
Vigneto/vignoble/viña	Italian/French/Spanish, meaning 'vineyard'.
Vin/vino	French/Italian and Spanish, meaning 'wine'.
Vinification	The process of making wine from grapes.
Vinosity	The distinctive colour, aroma and flavour of a wine.
Viticulture	The science of growing vines.
Winery	Where grapes are made into wine.
Yeast	A living organism that is found in, amongst other things, grape juice, and which reacts with the sugar in the grapes to produce alcohol and carbon dioxide during *Fermentation*.

INDEX

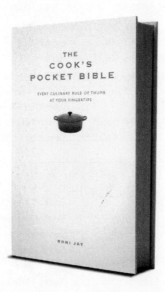